L. B. Shook

Shook's Song Evangelist

A new collection of music for Sunday schools, gospel meetings, choirs and private worship

L. B. Shook

Shook's Song Evangelist
A new collection of music for Sunday schools, gospel meetings, choirs and private worship

ISBN/EAN: 9783337286101

Printed in Europe, USA, Canada, Australia, Japan

Cover: Foto ©Lupo / pixelio.de

More available books at **www.hansebooks.com**

SHOOK'S SONG EVANGELIST.

A New Collection of Music

FOR

Sunday Schools, Gospel Meetings, Choirs
and Private Worship.

Written and Compiled

BY

L. B. SHOOK.

PUBLISHED BY

S. BRAINARD'S SONS,
CLEVELAND & CHICAGO.

PREFACE.

In the following collection of new, standard and favorite songs, hymn-tunes, etc., the author has aimed to supply the Sunday School, the Choir and Congregation, the Gospel Meeting and the Home Circle with a book that shall prove useful in every Christian community. The new songs for the Sabbath School are bright, cheerful, and appropriate to many of the favorite texts of the Bible. The collection of new hymns, as well as the old and beloved tunes, will be welcome in all religious meetings; and we hope that the "Song Evangelist" may go forth doing good—proving itself worthy of its name and aim.

THE AUTHOR AND PUBLISHERS.

COPYRIGHT 1883, S. BRAINARD'S SONS.

SONG EVANGELIST.

WE COME WITH HAPPY SONGS.

L. B. SHOOK.

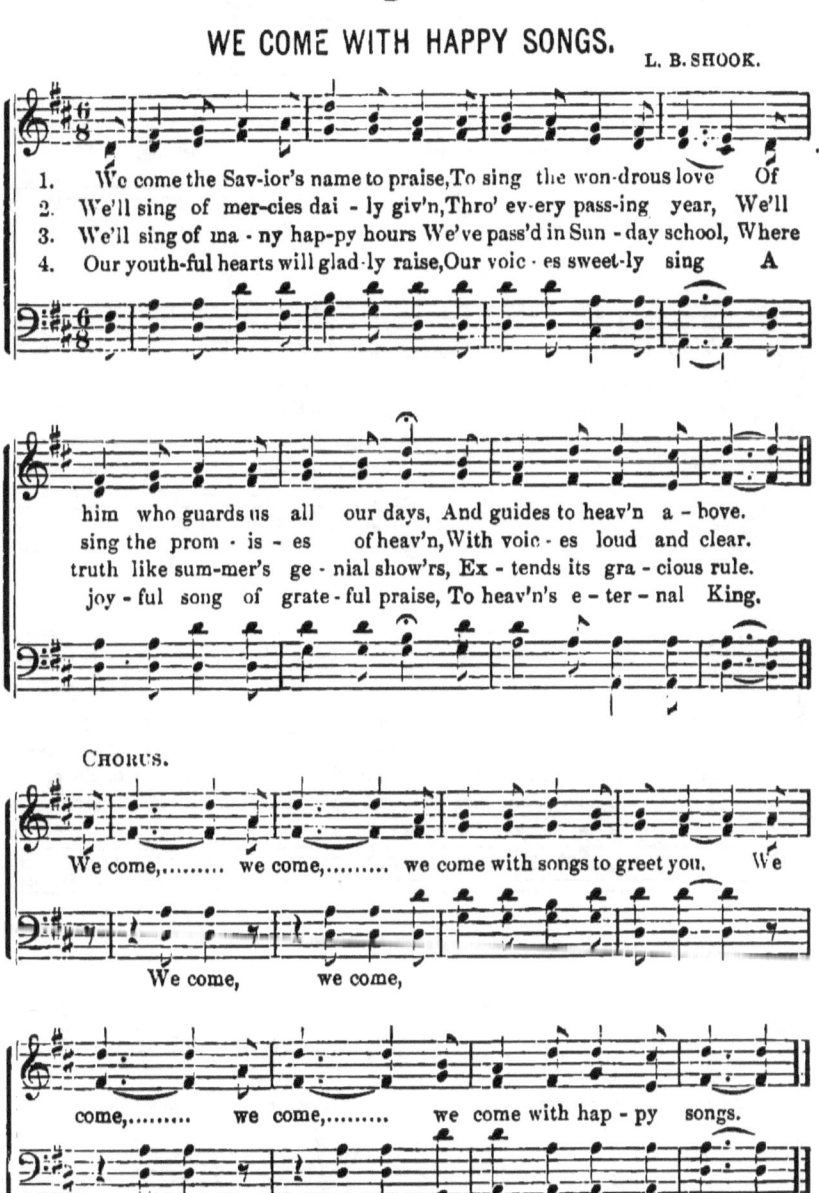

1. We come the Savior's name to praise, To sing the wondrous love Of him who guards us all our days, And guides to heav'n above.
2. We'll sing of mercies daily giv'n, Thro' every passing year, We'll sing the promises of heav'n, With voices loud and clear.
3. We'll sing of many happy hours We've pass'd in Sunday school, Where truth like summer's genial show'rs, Extends its gracious rule.
4. Our youthful hearts will gladly raise, Our voices sweetly sing A joyful song of grateful praise, To heav'n's eternal King.

CHORUS.

We come,......... we come,......... we come with songs to greet you. We come,......... we come,......... we come with happy songs.

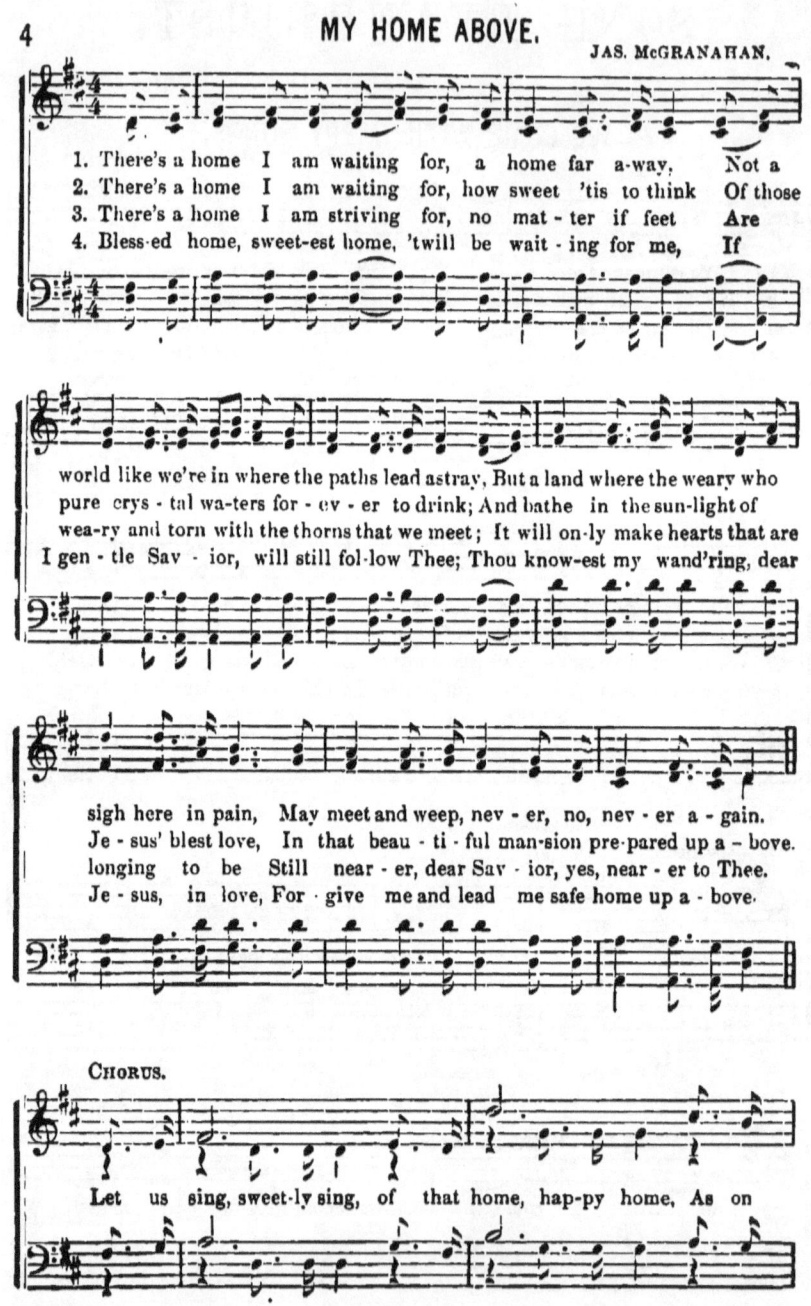

TRUST IN JESUS.—Concluded.

7

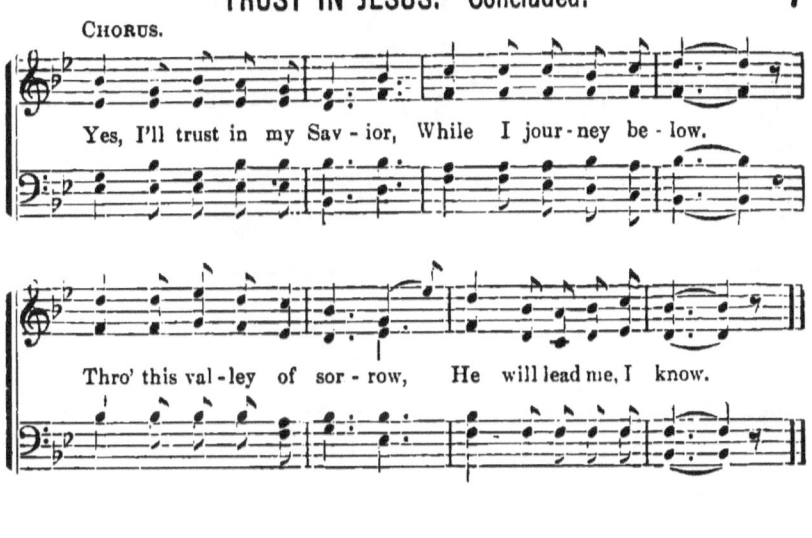

Yes, I'll trust in my Sav-ior, While I jour-ney be-low.
Thro' this val-ley of sor-row, He will lead me, I know.

UNION.

P. H. MONTAGUE.

1. Do not I love thee, O my Lord? Be-hold my heart and see,
2. Do not I love thee from my soul? Then let me noth-ing love.
3. Is not thy name me-lo-dious still To my at-ten-tive ear?
4. Thou knowest I love thee, dear-est Lord, But, O I long to soar

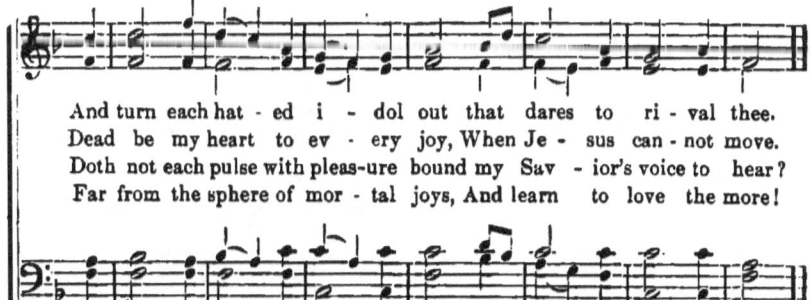

And turn each hat-ed i-dol out that dares to ri-val thee.
Dead be my heart to ev-ery joy, When Je-sus can-not move.
Doth not each pulse with pleas-ure bound my Sav-ior's voice to hear?
Far from the sphere of mor-tal joys, And learn to love the more!

NO NIGHT ON THAT GOLDEN SHORE.

L. B. SHOOK.

1. O when shall we sweet-ly re-move, O when shall we en-ter our rest,
2. But an-gels them-selves can-not tell The joys of that ho-li-est place

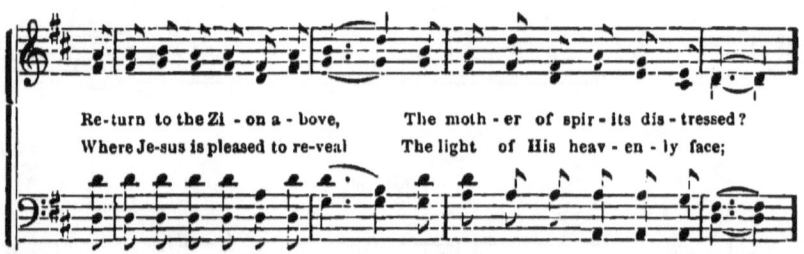

Re-turn to the Zi-on a-bove, The moth-er of spir-its dis-tressed?
Where Je-sus is pleased to re-veal The light of His heav-en-ly face;

The cit-y of God the great King, Where sor-row and death are no more,
When caught in the rapturous flame, The sight be-at-i-fic they prove;

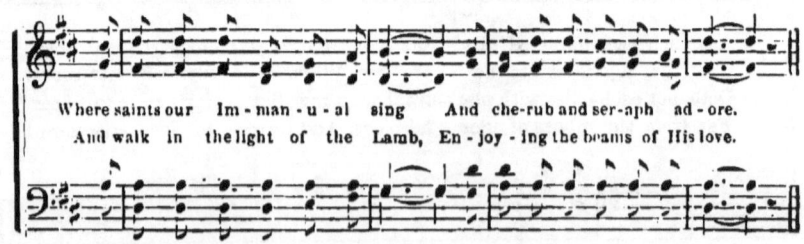

Where saints our Im-man-u-al sing And che-rub and ser-aph ad-ore.
And walk in the light of the Lamb, En-joy-ing the beams of His love.

NO NIGHT ON THAT GOLDEN SHORE.—Concluded.

CHORUS.

There is no night on that golden shore;
There is no night on that golden shore, There is no night on that golden shore;

There shall we suf - fer and sigh no more
There shall we suffer and sigh no more, There shall we suffer and sigh no more.

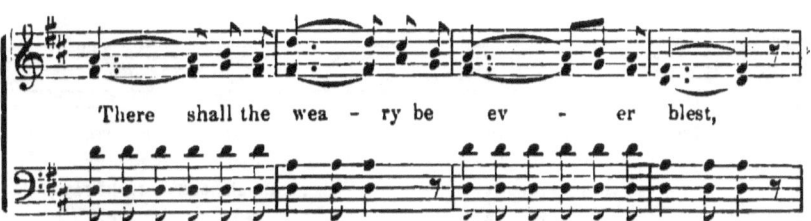

There shall the wea - ry be ev - er blest,
There shall the weary be ev-er blest, There shall the weary be ev - er blest,

Sing - ing glad songs in the land of sweet rest.
sweet rest.
Singing glad songs in the land of rest, Sing in the land of sweet rest.

BE STILL, MY HEART, AND WAIT.—Concluded.

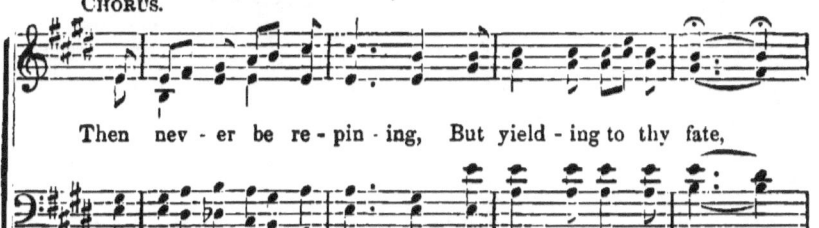

Then nev-er be re-pin-ing, But yield-ing to thy fate,

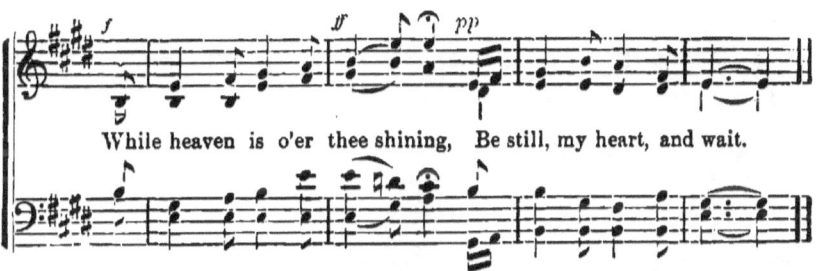

While heaven is o'er thee shining, Be still, my heart, and wait.

IT IS NOT DEATH TO DIE.
(FOR FUNERALS.)
L. B. SHOOK.

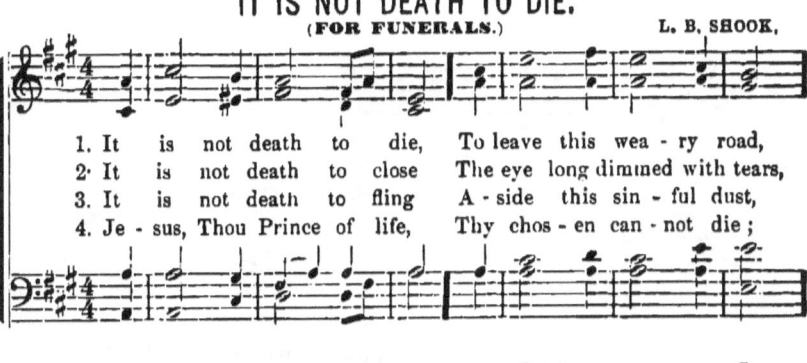

1. It is not death to die, To leave this wea-ry road,
2. It is not death to close The eye long dimmed with tears,
3. It is not death to fling A-side this sin-ful dust,
4. Je-sus, Thou Prince of life, Thy chos-en can-not die;

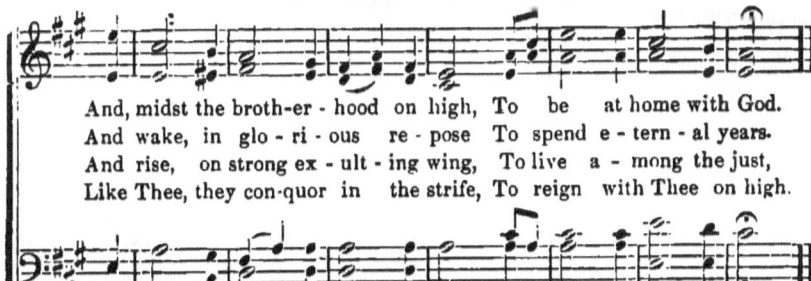

And, midst the broth-er-hood on high, To be at home with God.
And wake, in glo-ri-ous re-pose To spend e-tern-al years.
And rise, on strong ex-ult-ing wing, To live a-mong the just,
Like Thee, they con-quor in the strife, To reign with Thee on high.

LET ME TARRY AT THE FOUNTAIN.—Concluded.

foun-tain where the sparkling wa-ter free-ly flows; In the pres-ence of my Sav-ior may I al-ways stay, Drinking deep of the fount of life.

TRANSIENT.

REV. KIT WILLIAMS.   L. B. SHOOK.

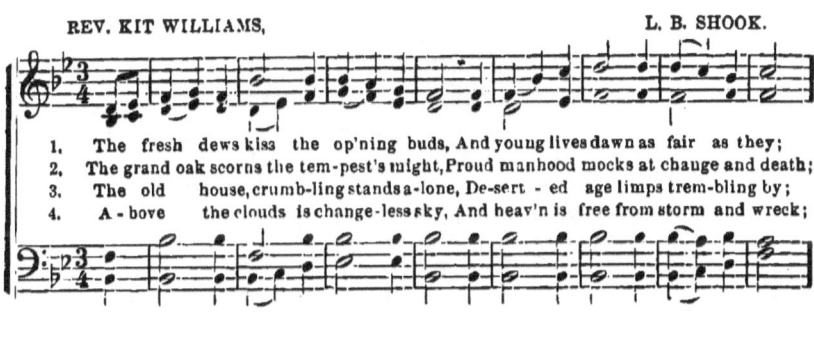

1. The fresh dews kiss the op'ning buds, And young lives dawn as fair as they;
2. The grand oak scorns the tem-pest's might, Proud manhood mocks at change and death;
3. The old house, crumb-ling stands a-lone, De-sert - ed age limps trem-bling by;
4. A-bove the clouds is change-less sky, And heav'n is free from storm and wreck;

The sun-set falls on fad - ed flow'rs, Fond youth-dreams fade as soon a-way.
The bolt in shiv - ers rends the oak, In fear the strong man yields his breath.
O wea - ry length of change-ful years, Your hopes were on - ly born to die!
How safe the hopes that an - chor there, Where fade - less crowns the saints be-deck.

TEMPERANCE SONG.

L. B. SHOOK.

1. We wage a might-y war, boys, A-gainst a might-y foe, Who thro' the land with bus-y hand, Is spreading want and woe; He's sadden'd many a light heart, And many a thous-and slain, Then
2. Our poor-hous-es are filled, boys, With paupers drink has made, The cash which would sup-port them, boys, To gin-shops has been paid; And we've these poor to suc-cor, boys, Though naught we have to spare; The
3. If strong drink from the land, boys, Was swept a-way to-night, Some of our pris-on hous-es Would close their por-tals quite; And one half of the po-lice, force For which we're tax'ed to pay, With-

TEMPERANCE SONG.—Concluded.

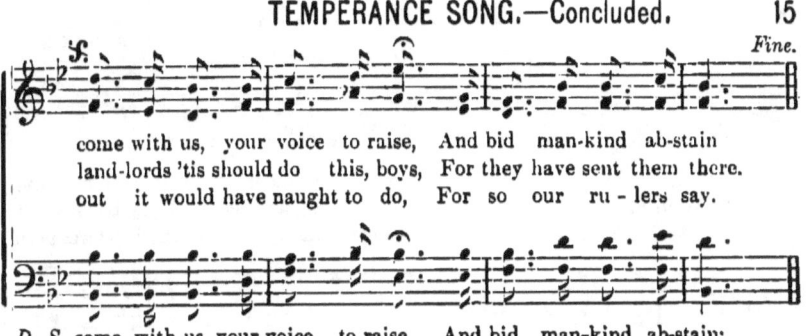

come with us, your voice to raise, And bid man-kind ab-stain
land-lords 'tis should do this, boys, For they have sent them there.
out it would have naught to do, For so our ru - lers say.

D. S. come with us, your voice to raise, And bid man-kind ab-stain:

We wage a might - y war, boys, A -

gainst a might - y foe, Who thro' the land, with

bu - sy hand, Is spread-ing want and woe. Then

OUR SAVIOR'S NAME.

To Rev. G. W. SMITH, Gonzales, Texas.

L. B. SHOOK.

1. Our Savior's name, our Savior's name, O, sound it forth with loud ac-claim;
2. With viol, harp, and trumpets sound, Now let the festal joy be crowned:
3. Blest be the ev-er sacred morn, That shrines the joy when Christ was born:

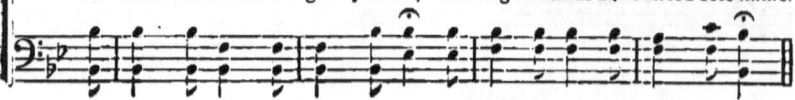

While heav'n and earth in con-cert sing, Su-blim-est strains of praise to bring.
While all on earth re-joice a-gain, And sing in sweet, triumphant strain.
When He from realms of glo-ry came, And ang-el bands announced His name.

CHORUS.

O wreathe it in cho — ral strain; With peace on
Wreathe it in sweet choral strain, Wreathe it in sweet choral strain,

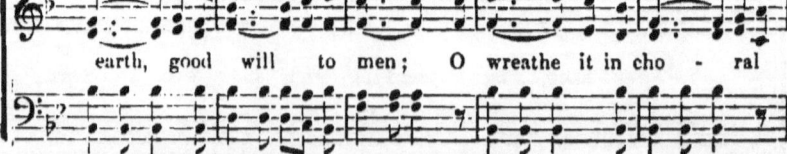

earth, good will to men; O wreathe it in cho - ral
Peace on earth, good will to men, good will to men; Wreathe it in sweet choral strain,

OUR SAVIOR'S NAME.—Concluded.

strain, with peace on earth, good will to men.

Wreathe it in sweet choral strain, Peace on earth, good will, good will to men.

TELL JESUS.

"YOUTH'S COMPANION." L. B. SHOOK.

Not too fast.

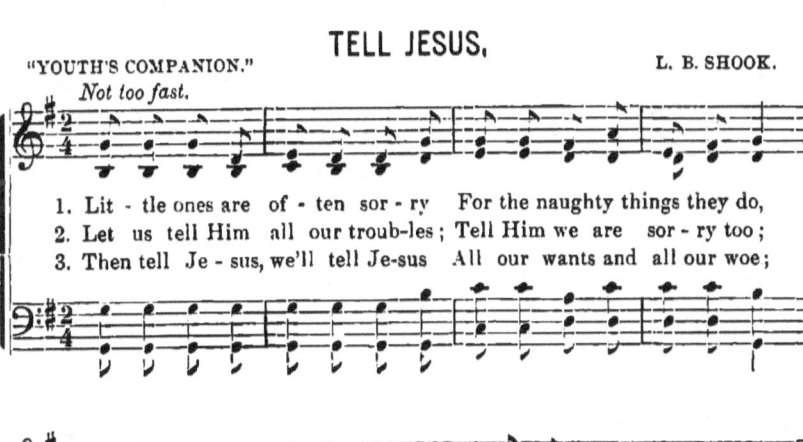

1. Lit - tle ones are of - ten sor - ry   For the naughty things they do,
2. Let us tell Him all our troub-les;   Tell Him we are sor - ry too;
3. Then tell Je - sus, we'll tell Je-sus   All our wants and all our woe;

Sor-rows reach us all, and trou - ble Lit-tle hearts and big ones too.
He will do us kind-ness, dou-ble, Help us to be good and true,
None but Je - sus can re - lieve us, None but Je - sus love us so.

REFRAIN.

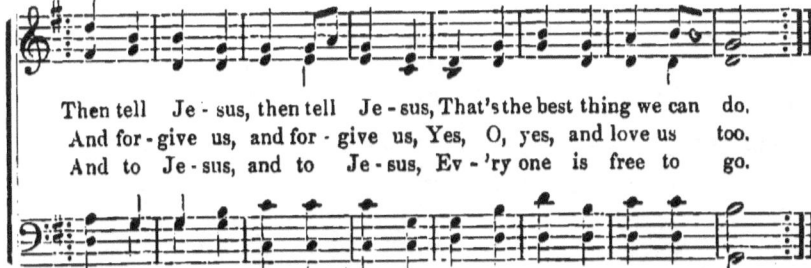

Then tell Je - sus, then tell Je - sus, That's the best thing we can do.
And for - give us, and for - give us, Yes, O, yes, and love us too.
And to Je - sus, and to Je - sus, Ev - 'ry one is free to go.

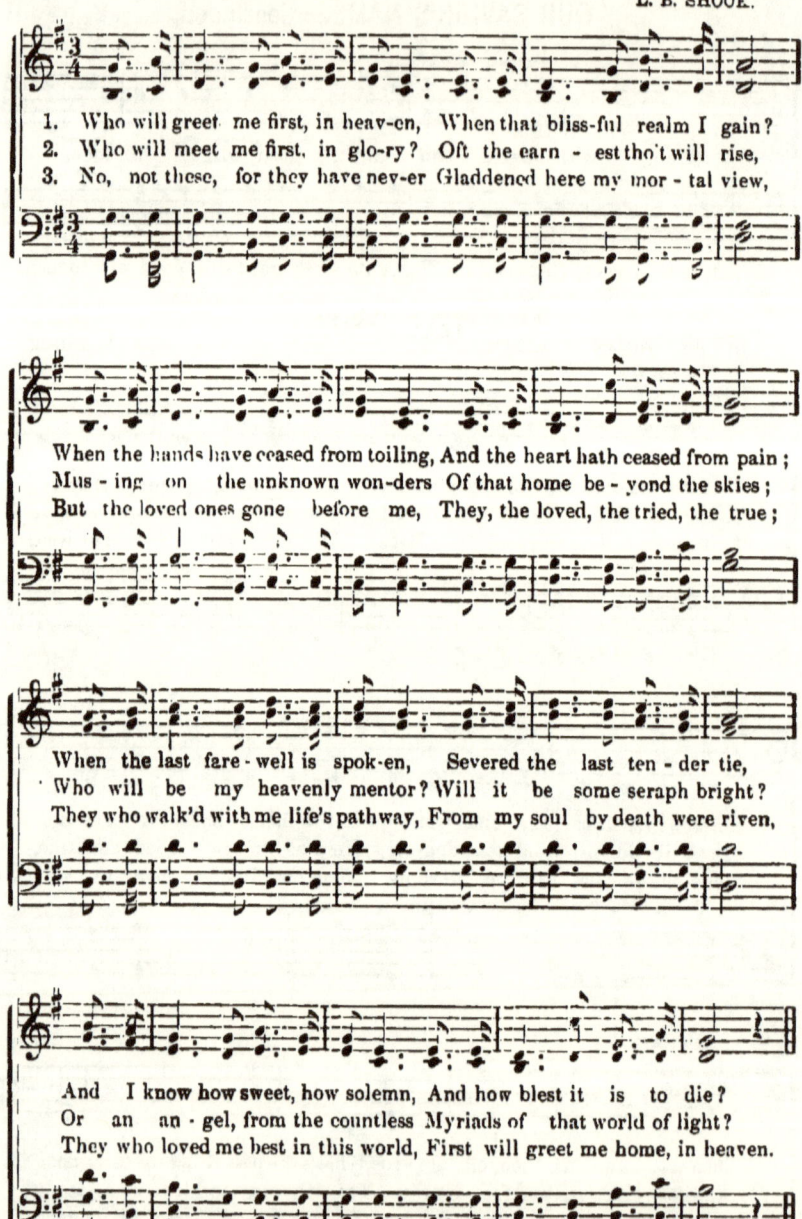

WHO WILL GREET ME FIRST IN HEAVEN?—Concluded.

CHORUS.

Home, sweet home, That home so bright and fair; O,
Home, sweet home, O, home, sweet home,

Home, sweet home, O who will greet me there?
Home, sweet home, O, home, sweet home,

HOLLAND.
ALLIE L. SMITH.

1. Far from mor-tal cares retreating, Sordid hopes, and vain desires, Here, our
2. From the fount of glo-ry beaming, Light ce-les-tial cheers our eyes, Mer-cy
3. Who may share this great salva-tion? Ev-ery pure and humble mind, Ev-ery
4. Blessings all around bestowing, God withholds his care from none, Grace and

will - ing foot-steps meet - ing, Ev - ery heart to heav'n as - pires.
from a - bove pro-claim - ing, Peace and par - don from the skies.
kin-dred, tongue, and na - tion, From the stains of guilt re - fin'd.
mer - cy ev - er flow - ing, From the foun - tain of his throne.

VAUGHN.

DANIEL P. AIRHART.

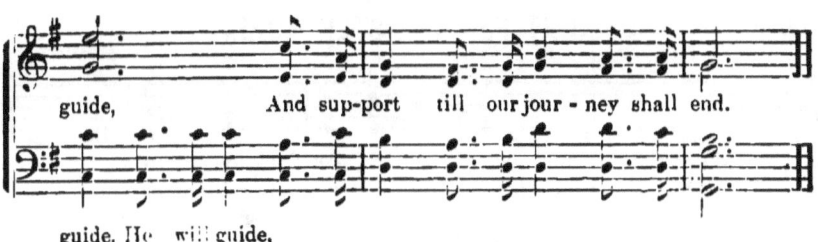

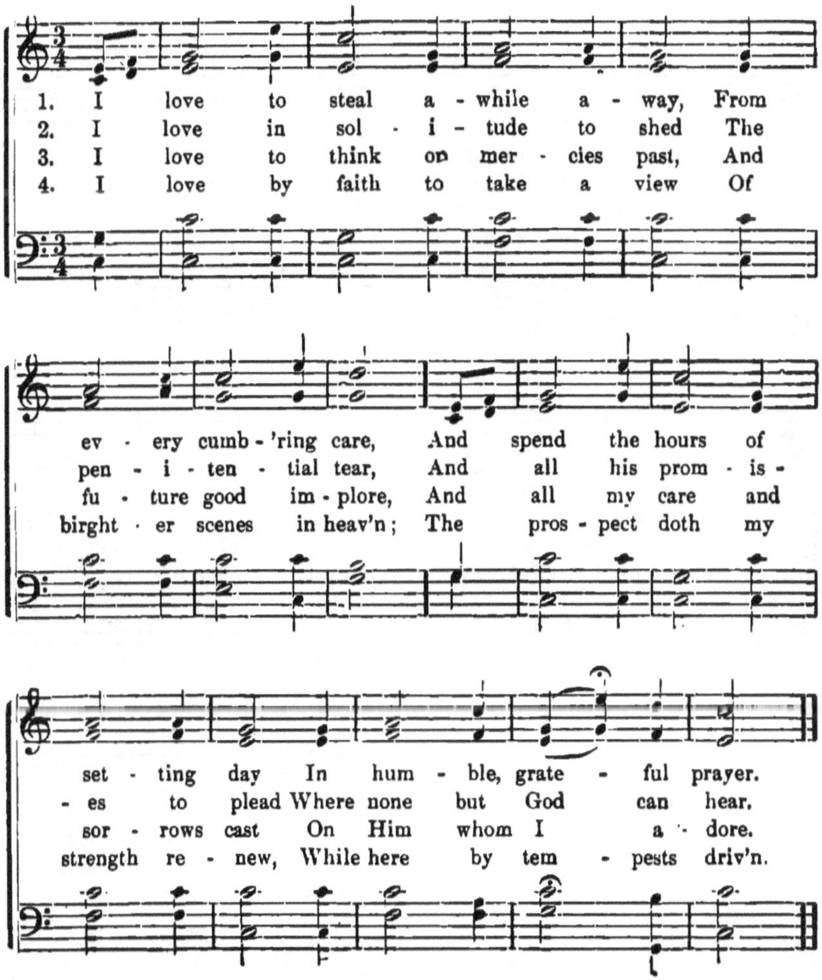

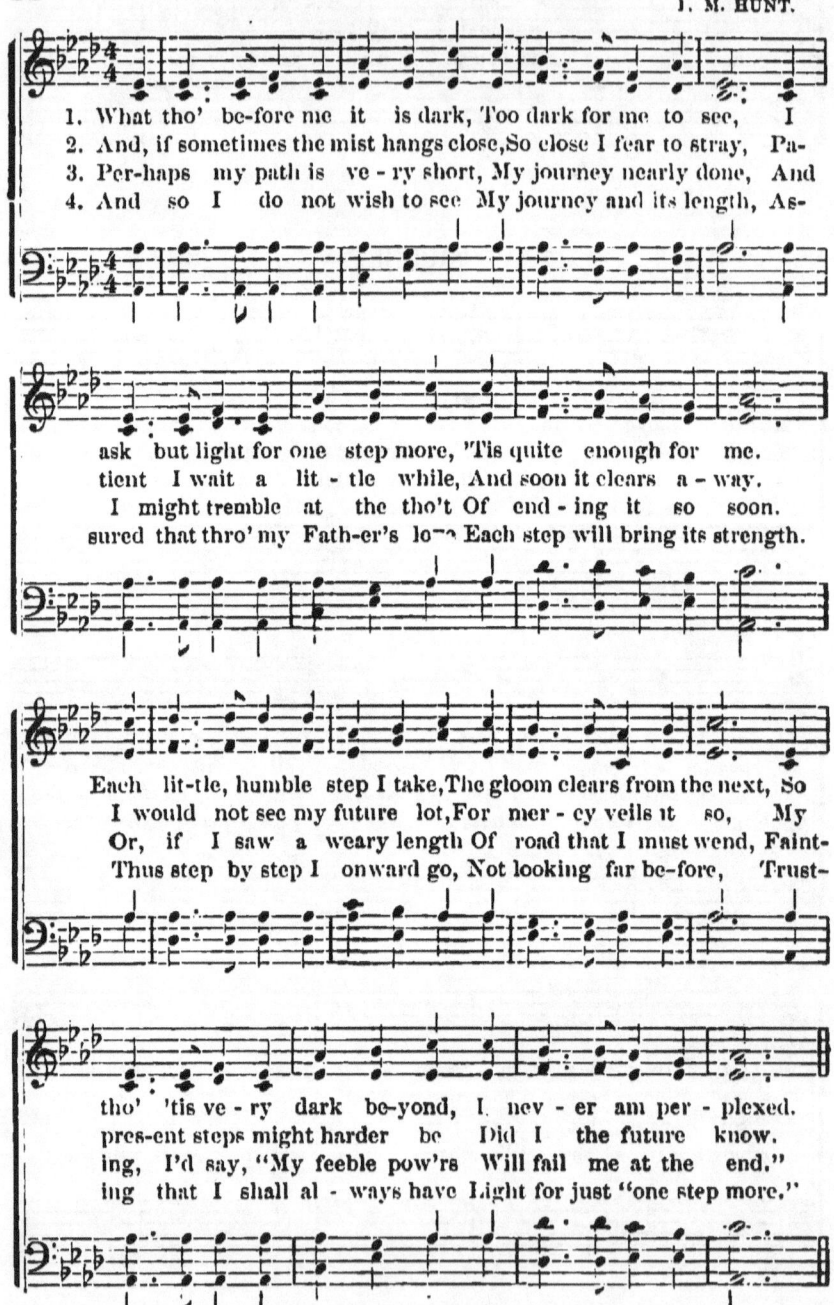

LIGHT FOR ONE STEP MORE.—Concluded.

CHORUS.

One step more, One step more, Give me light for one step more.
Light for one step more, Light for one step more,
One step more, One step more, Light for one step more.
Light for one step more, Light for one step more.

Mc CREARY.

ALLIE L. SMITH.

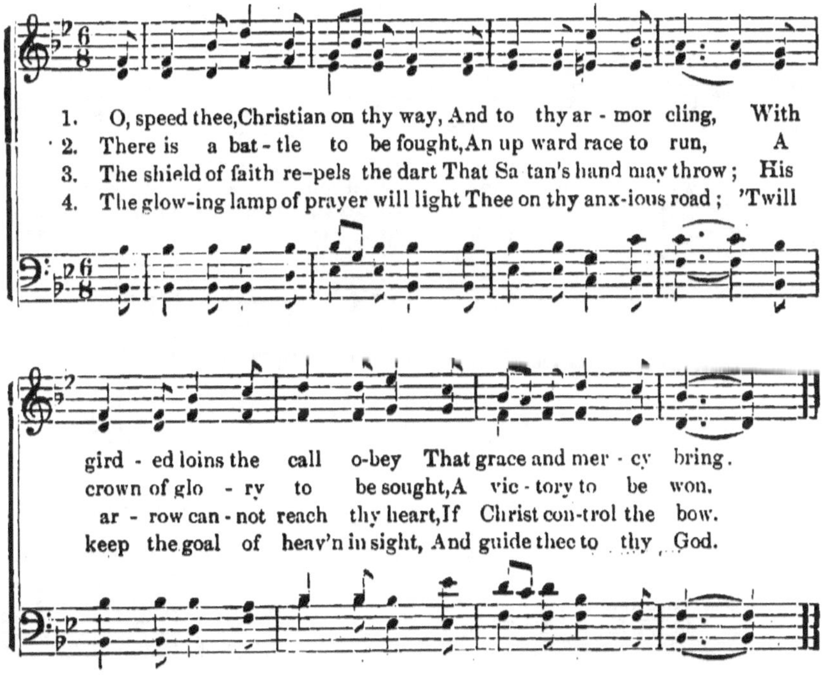

1. O, speed thee, Christian on thy way, And to thy ar-mor cling, With
2. There is a bat-tle to be fought, An up ward race to run, A
3. The shield of faith re-pels the dart That Satan's hand may throw; His
4. The glow-ing lamp of prayer will light Thee on thy anx-ious road; 'Twill

gird-ed loins the call o-bey That grace and mer-cy bring.
crown of glo-ry to be sought, A vic-to-ry to be won.
ar-row can-not reach thy heart, If Christ con-trol the bow.
keep the goal of heav'n in sight, And guide thee to thy God.

REST.—Concluded.

Come rest, come rest, Thou faith - ful one,
Come rest, come rest, O, faithful one, Thou faithful one, come rest at home.

There's rest for thee, sweet rest at home.
Thou'lt hear the Master say 'well done, there's rest for thee at home.

FRESNO.

SIR JOHN BROWNING.   L. B. SHOOK.

1. God is love: his mer-cy brightens All the path in which we rove;
2. Death and change are bu-sy ev-er, Man de-cays and a-ges move;
3. E'en the hour that darkest seemeth Will his changeless goodness prove;
4. He with earthly cares entwineth Hope and comfort from a-bove;

Bliss he wakes, and woe he lightens, God is wisdom, God is love.
But His mercy waneth never: God is wisdom, God is love.
From the gloom his brightness streameth: God is wisdom, God is love.
Ev - ery - where his glo - ry shineth: God is wisdom, God is love.

OPEN THE DOOR FOR THE CHILDREN.

L. B. SHOOK.

1. O-pen the door for the children, Ten-der-ly gather them in;
2. O-pen the door for the children, See, they are coming in throngs,
3. O-pen the door for the children, Take the dear lambs by the hand,

In from the highways and hedg-es, In from the plac-es of sin;
Bid them sit down at the banquet, Teach them your beau-ti-ful songs,
Point them to truth and to Je-sus, Point them to heaven's bright land.

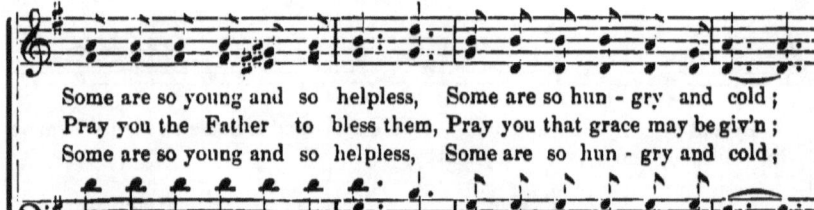

Some are so young and so helpless, Some are so hun-gry and cold;
Pray you the Father to bless them, Pray you that grace may be giv'n;
Some are so young and so helpless, Some are so hun-gry and cold;

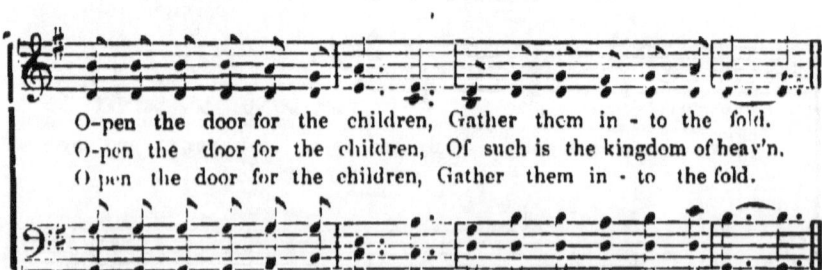

O-pen the door for the children, Gather them in-to the fold.
O-pen the door for the children, Of such is the kingdom of heav'n.
O-pen the door for the children, Gather them in-to the fold.

OPEN THE DOOR FOR THE CHILDREN.—Concluded.

CHORUS.

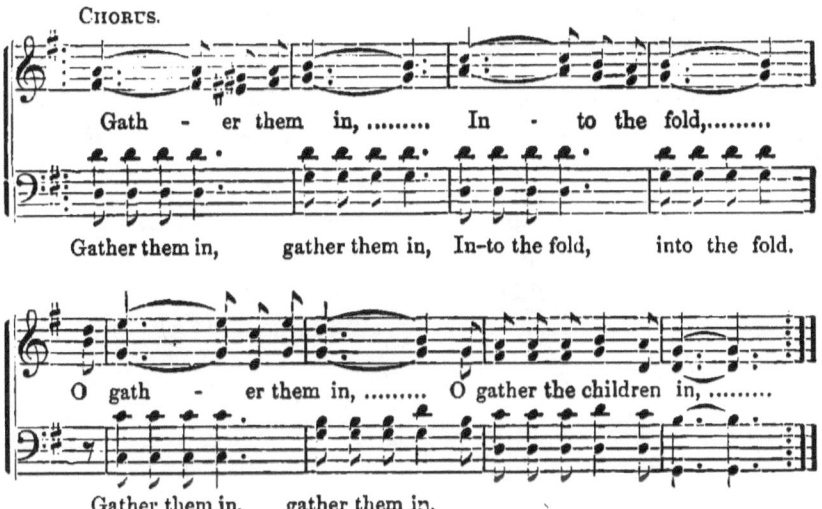

Gath - er them in, ... In - to the fold, ...
Gather them in, gather them in, In-to the fold, into the fold.

O gath - er them in, ... O gather the children in, ...
Gather them in, gather them in,

MORNING PRAYER.

L. B. SHOOK.

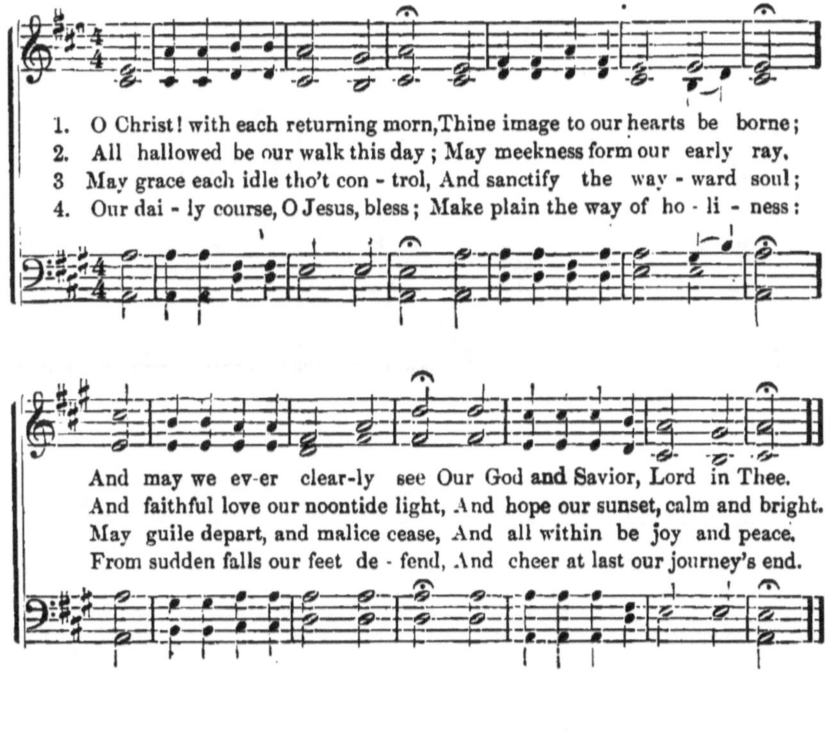

1. O Christ! with each returning morn, Thine image to our hearts be borne;
2. All hallowed be our walk this day; May meekness form our early ray,
3. May grace each idle tho't con - trol, And sanctify the way - ward soul;
4. Our dai - ly course, O Jesus, bless; Make plain the way of ho - li - ness:

And may we ev-er clear-ly see Our God and Savior, Lord in Thee.
And faithful love our noontide light, And hope our sunset, calm and bright.
May guile depart, and malice cease, And all within be joy and peace.
From sudden falls our feet de - fend, And cheer at last our journey's end.

REMEMBER THE SAVIOR.

MRS. T. M. GRIFFIN.   L. B. SHOOK.

"*Remember thy Creator, in the days of thy youth, while the evil days come not.*" — Ecl. 12; 1.

1. Tho' the sun-shine in beau-ty a-dorn thy young day, And the radiance of pleas-ure il -
2. Let thy heart's purest treasure be giv - en to Him, Ere the e - vil o'er take thee or
3. Ere the sunbeams by sorrow be driv-en a-way; Ere the radiance of pleas-ure be-

lumes the whole way, Tho' the dark shades of sor - row a-way from thee flee, O, for -
faith be-comes dim, To the Sav-ior who suf-fered in sor-row and woe, Let thy
dim'd by de - cay; Ere the storm clouds of an-guish up-on thee shall break, O, re-

CHORUS.

get not the Sav - ior who died once for thee. For thee,   for
tru - est de - vo - tion and soul-yearn-ing flow,
mem-ber the Sav - ior who died for thy sake.   for thee,

thee,   O, remember the Sav-ior, who died once for thee; For thee,   for
for thee,   for thee,

REMEMBER THE SAVIOR.—Concluded.

thee, O, re-mem-ber the Sav-ior, who died once for thee.
thee, for thee,

SAVIOR LEAD US ALL THE WAY.

"And the street of the city was pure gold, as it were transparent glass."—Rev. 21 ; 21.

MRS. T. M. GRIFFIN.   L. B. SHOOK.

1. Sav-ior lead us all the way; Nev-er let us go a-stray;
2. Teach-us how some soul to win; Give us strength to con-quer sin;
3. Give us pa-tience sweet and rare, All our grief and pain to bear;
4. Fath-er, to thy name a-bove, Source of peace and joy and love,

Keep us ev-er near Thy side, Al-ways be our shield and guide.
Let our hearts de-vot-ed be, Labor-ing Je-sus, here for thee.
To our hearts come woe or weal, Grant we naught but love may feel.
Let our hearts glad trib-ute bring; Let our loud ho-san-nas ring.

CHORUS.

Till our happy, happy feet, Tread with joy the golden street.

Till our hap-py, hap-py. feet, tread with joy the golden street.

34. ON THE BANKS OF THAT BRIGHT RIVER. *

MRS. T. M GRIFFIN. L. B. SHOOK.

And He showed me a pure river of water of life, as clear as crystal. Rev. 22: 1.

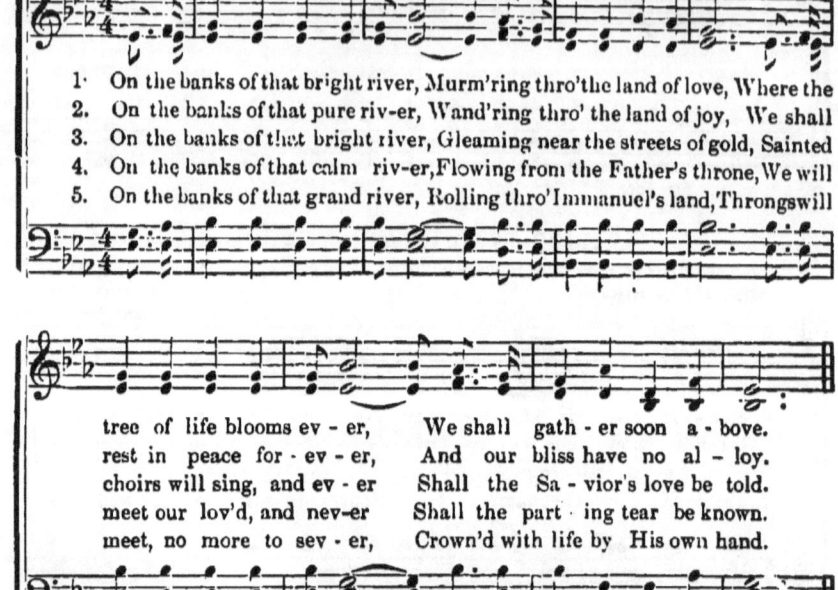

1. On the banks of that bright river, Murm'ring thro' the land of love, Where the tree of life blooms ev-er, We shall gath-er soon a-bove.
2. On the banks of that pure riv-er, Wand'ring thro' the land of joy, We shall rest in peace for-ev-er, And our bliss have no al-loy.
3. On the banks of that bright river, Gleaming near the streets of gold, Sainted choirs will sing, and ev-er Shall the Sa-vior's love be told.
4. On the banks of that calm riv-er, Flowing from the Father's throne, We will meet our lov'd, and nev-er Shall the part-ing tear be known.
5. On the banks of that grand river, Rolling thro' Immanuel's land, Throngs will meet, no more to sev-er, Crown'd with life by His own hand.

CHORUS.

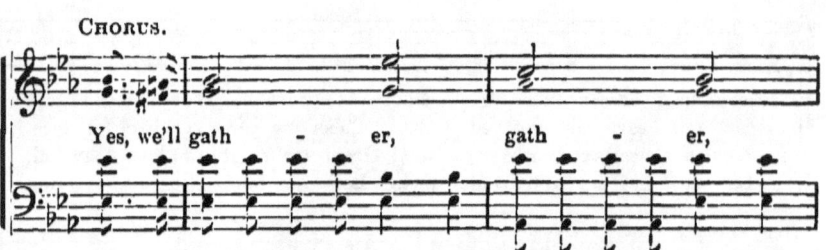

Yes, we'll gath - er, gath - er,
Yes, we'll gath - er, gath - er, gath - er, gath - er, gath - er, gath - er,

Gather 'round the throne above; Where lifes riv - er
Gather 'round the Father's throne above; Where life's river floweth, floweth,

*By per. "Alamo Music House," San Antonio, Texas.

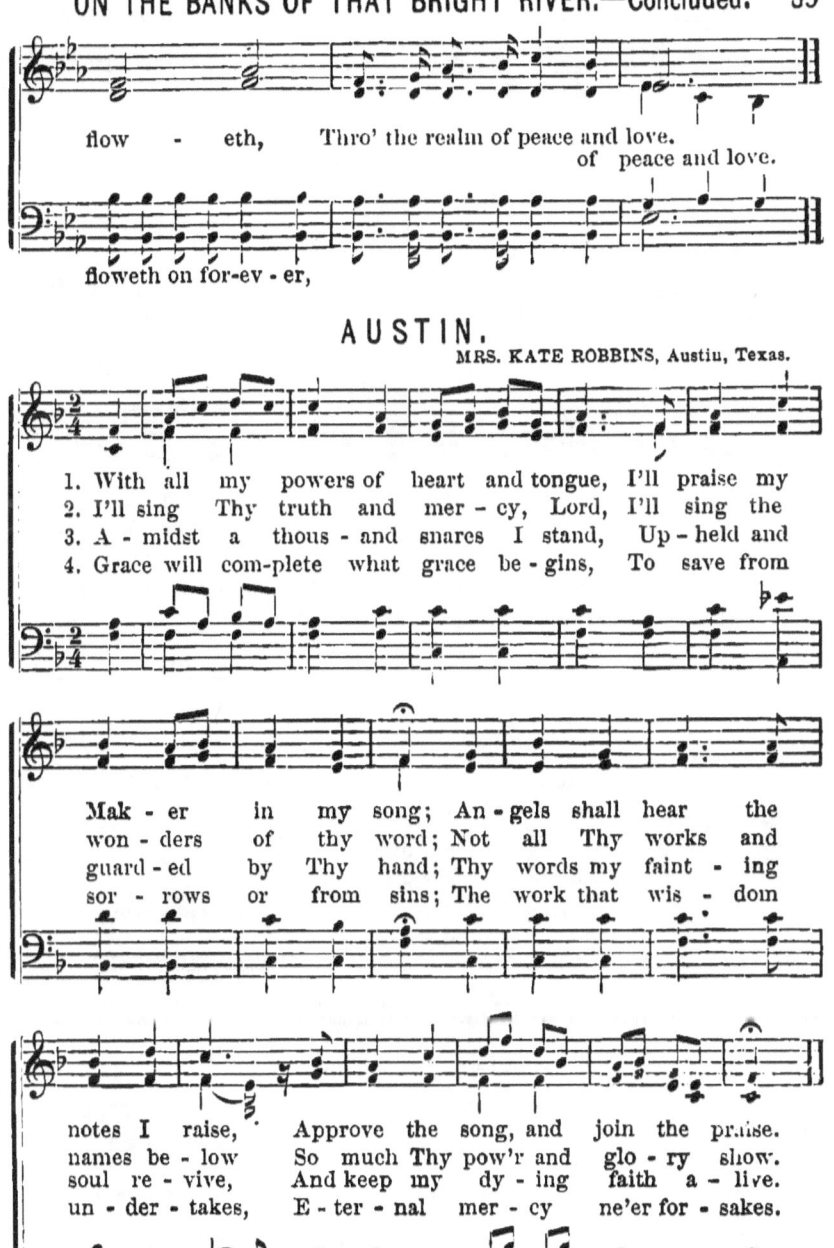

To Mrs C. F. PENN, Palestine, Texas.

REV. KIT. WILLIAMS. L. B. SHOOK.

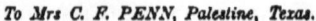

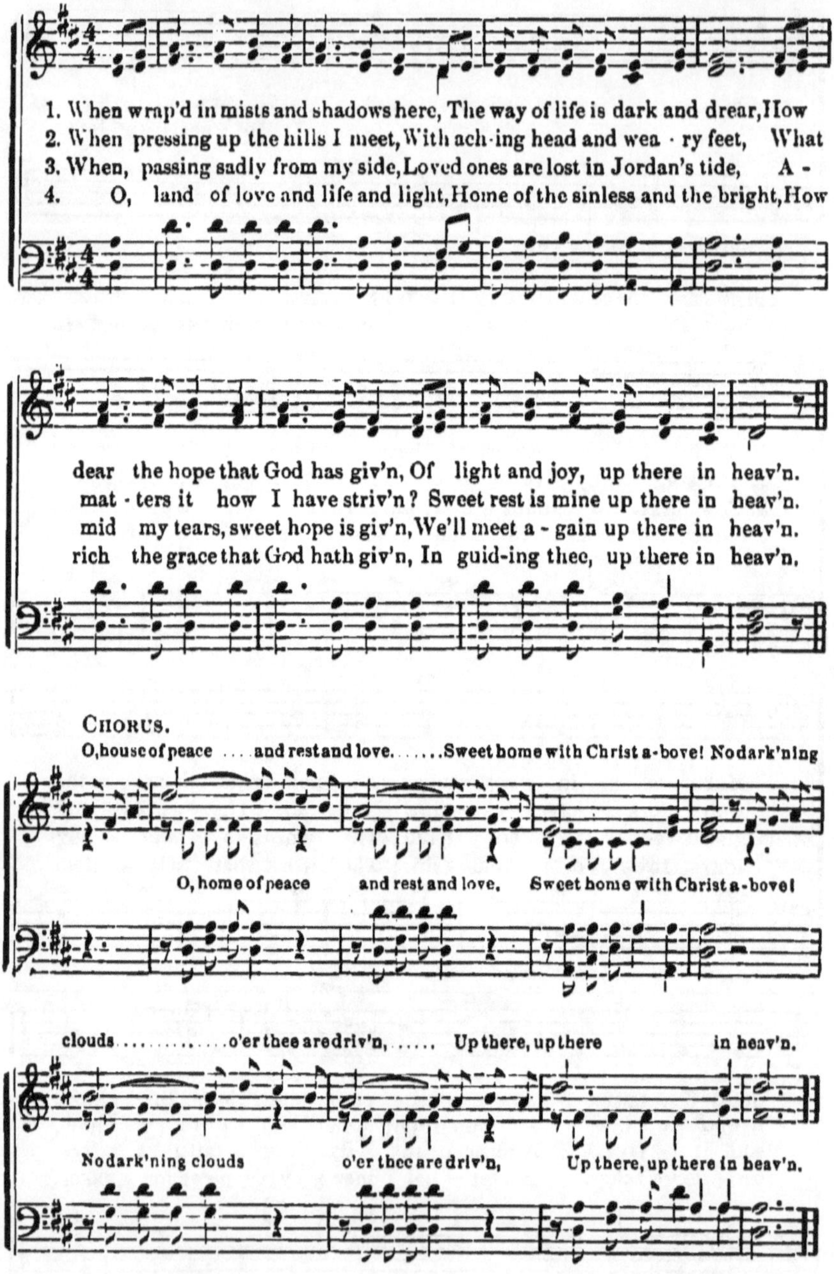
1. When wrap'd in mists and shadows here, The way of life is dark and drear, How
2. When pressing up the hills I meet, With ach-ing head and wea - ry feet, What
3. When, passing sadly from my side, Loved ones are lost in Jordan's tide, A -
4. O, land of love and life and light, Home of the sinless and the bright, How
dear the hope that God has giv'n, Of light and joy, up there in heav'n.
mat - ters it how I have striv'n? Sweet rest is mine up there in heav'n.
mid my tears, sweet hope is giv'n, We'll meet a - gain up there in heav'n.
rich the grace that God hath giv'n, In guid-ing thee, up there in heav'n.
CHORUS.
O, house of peace .... and rest and love...... Sweet home with Christ a-bove! No dark'ning
O, home of peace and rest and love, Sweet home with Christ a-bove!
clouds .... o'er thee are driv'n, ... Up there, up there in heav'n.
No dark'ning clouds o'er thee are driv'n, Up there, up there in heav'n.

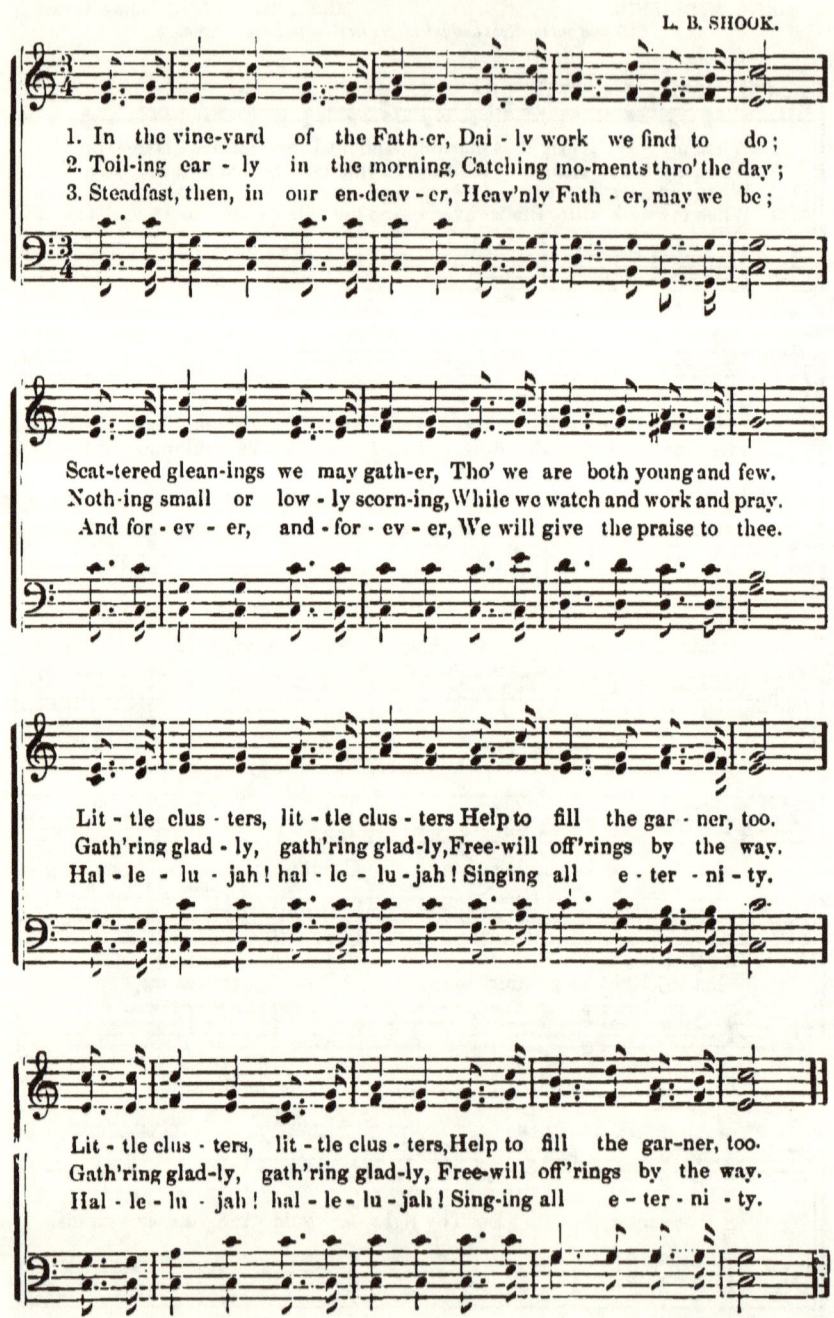

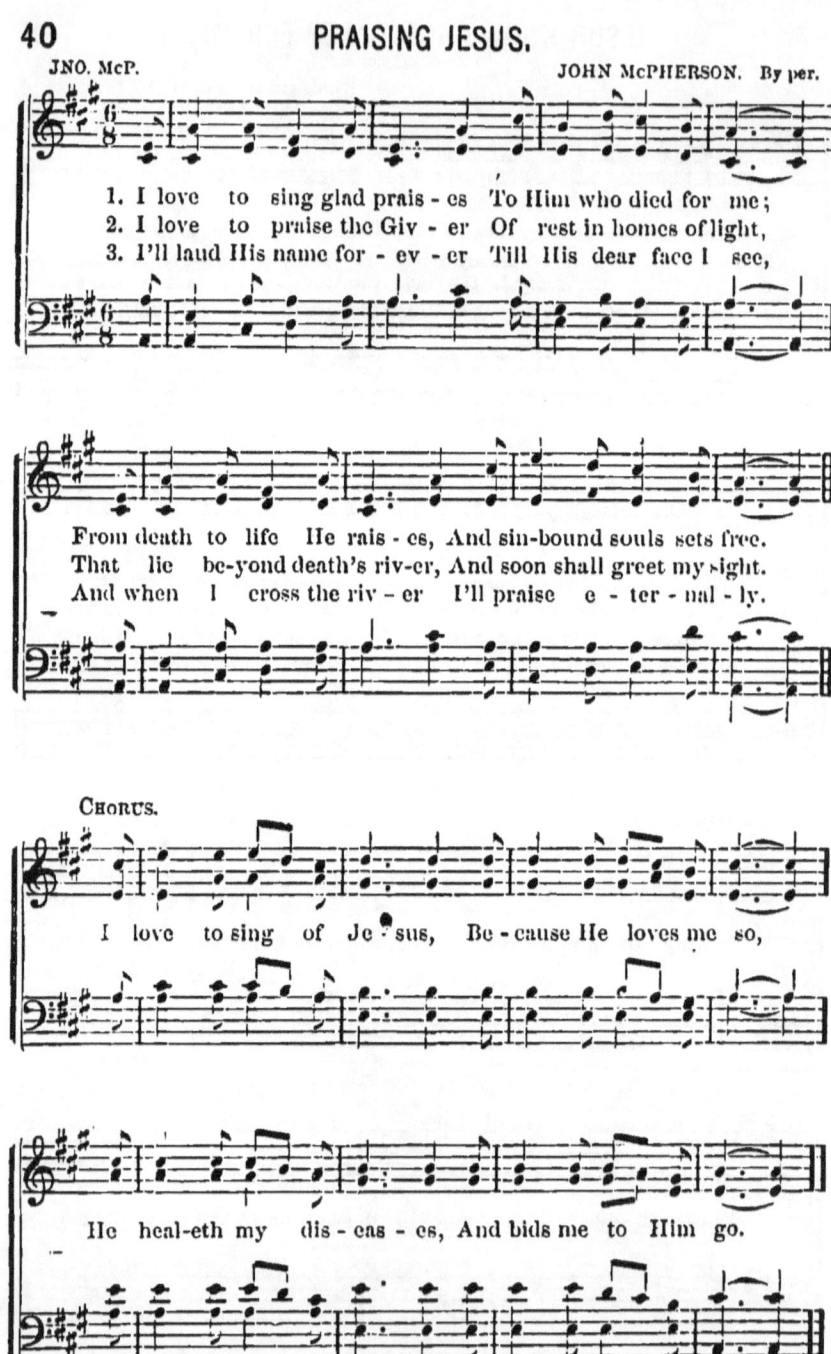

WE ARE COMING.

C. E. LESLIE. *by per.* 41

1. We have heard thy gentle voice, O blessed Sav-ior! We are coming, we are coming at thy
2. We will follow in thy footsteps, blessd Master, From thy paths of love and duty never
3. We will follow, tho' the tempest burst around us, Tho' the waves of earthly sorrow o'er us

call; Take us in thy mighty arms and help us ever, Safely shelter, in thy arms we fall.
stray; And thy loving voice shall cheer us as we journey To the land of beauty far a-way!
roll; For we know thy mighty hand will part the waters, And thy peace will still the storm control.

CHORUS.

We are com - - ing, we are com - ing, We are
Coming, coming, coming, Coming, coming, coming,

coming, blessed Savior, at thy call; We are com - ing,
Coming, coming, coming,
at thy call,

We are com - ing, We are safe when in thy mighty arms we fall.
coming, coming, coming,

OH, HEART, WAS IT IN VAIN?

"Little children, keep yourselves from idols." — John 5; 21.

MRS. T. M. GRIFFIN. J. M. HUNT.

1. O! heart, what is it makes thee stay A-way from Jesus true and kind? What burn-ing love hath o'er thee sway, That makes thee to His love so blind? What Siren-song doth woo thine ear, With earthly strains, so near sublime, That thy poor soul can nev-er hear The pleading voice of love di-vine.

2. O! heart, what hast thou placed above Thy ve-ry soul's e-ter-nal bliss? Is't wealth, or pride, or human love, That charms thee with a world like this? The gleaming gold will pass a-way, And fame become a mournful sound; Our hu-man loves are frail as clay, And oft-en bring us mortal wound.

3. Then heart what is it makes thee turn In coldness from the Savior's call? Some day His love may cease to yearn, And thou be left in sin's dark thrall; That i-dol priz'd by thee, so dear, O, nev-er, nev-er more enthrone, If thou would'st have the Lord draw near, To claim and bless thee as His own.

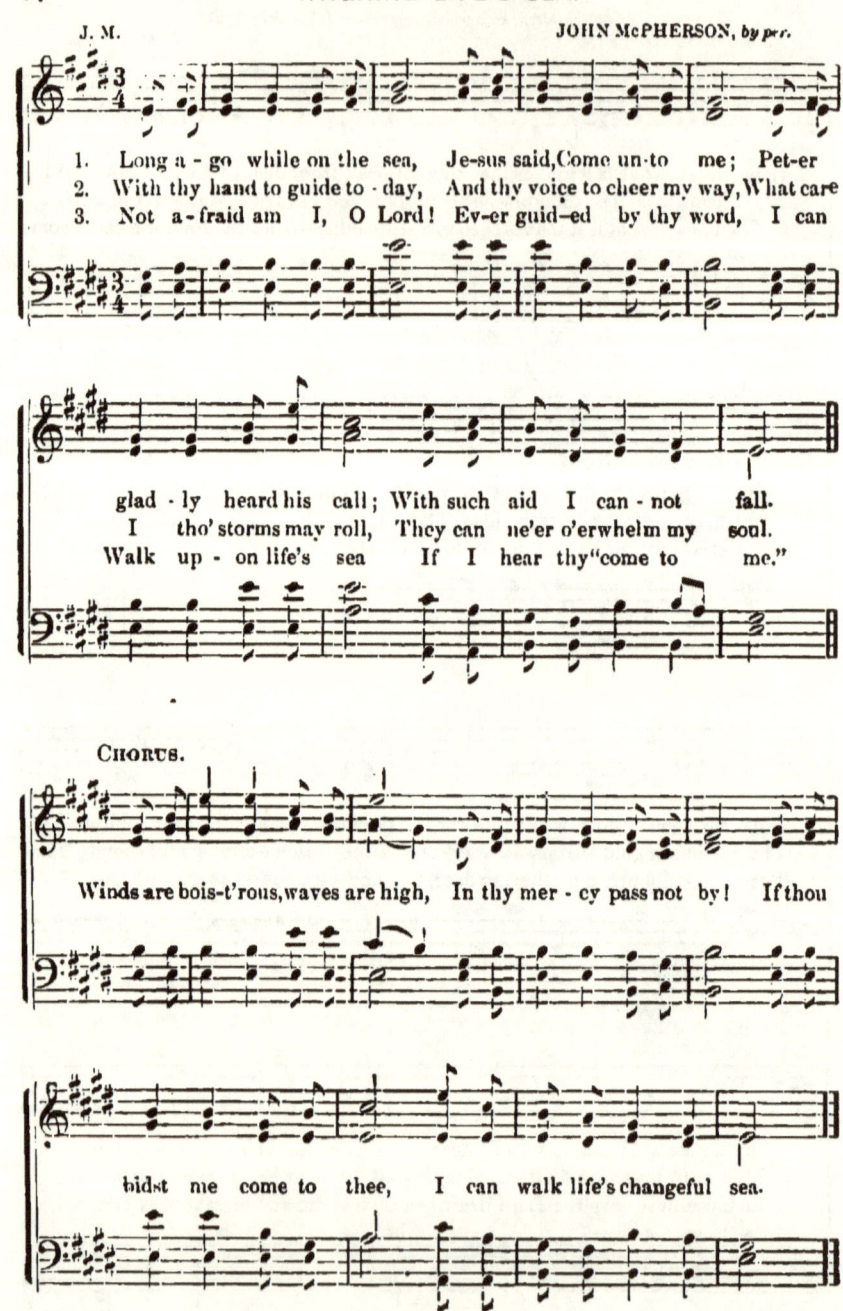

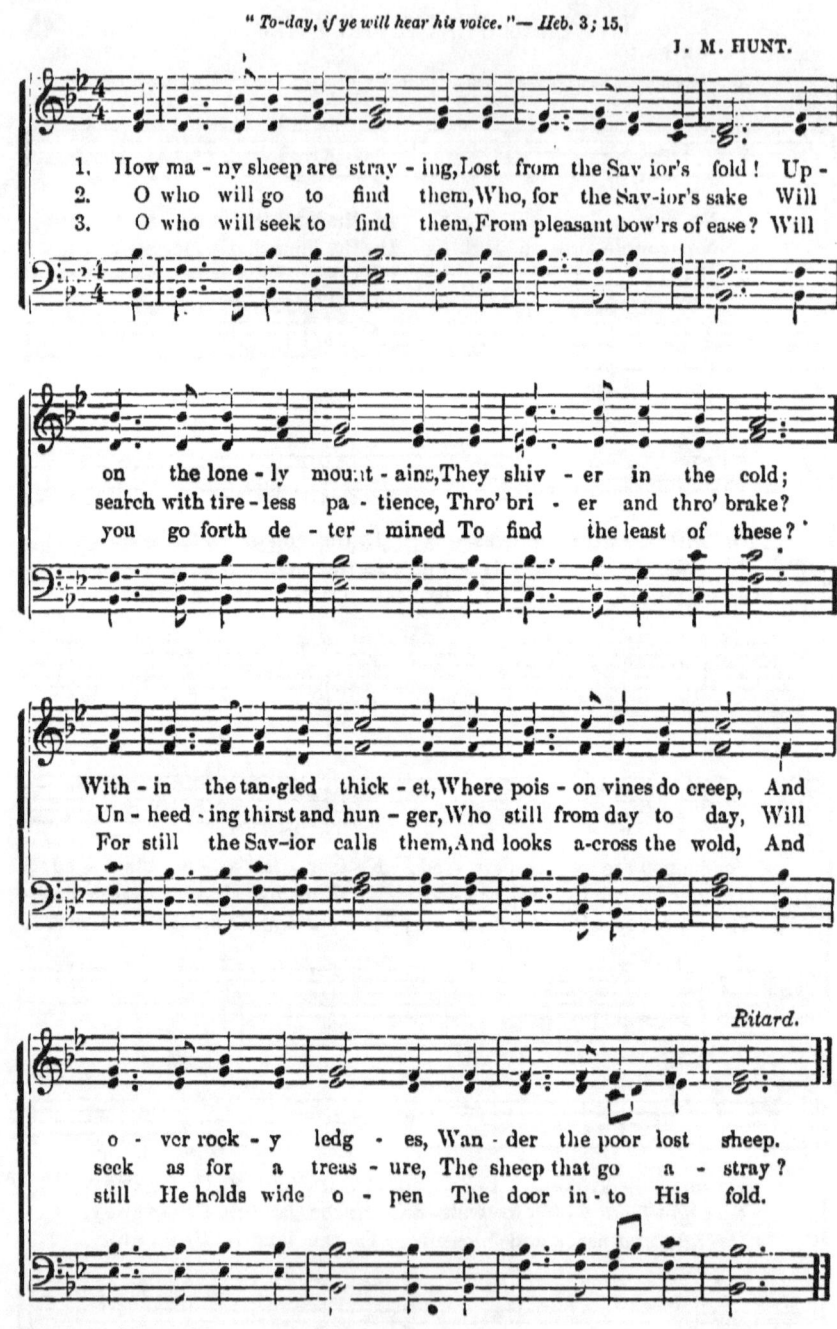

48   STAY, WEARY CHILD. *

R. A. GLENN   CHARLES EDW. POLLOCK.

1. Stay, weary child, the Savior calls, O turn and hear His gentle voice;
2. O hear the loving voice that calls, Forsake the dearest paths of sin,
3. Then, weary child, to Jesus come, All weak and helpless as thou art,

Come, now, to Him be reconciled, And He will bid thy heart rejoice.
For at the gates of mercy, now, The Savior waits to let thee in.
Thy burden to the Savior bring And He will cheer thy drooping heart.

CHORUS.

O, hear the Savior's voice; He's
Hear the Savior's voice, Hear the Savior's voice, He's

calling, now, to thee; O, make Him now your
calling now to thee, He's calling now to thee. Make Him now thy choice,

choice, He offers pardon, full and free.

Make Him now thy choice,

* From *Beauty of Praise*, by per.

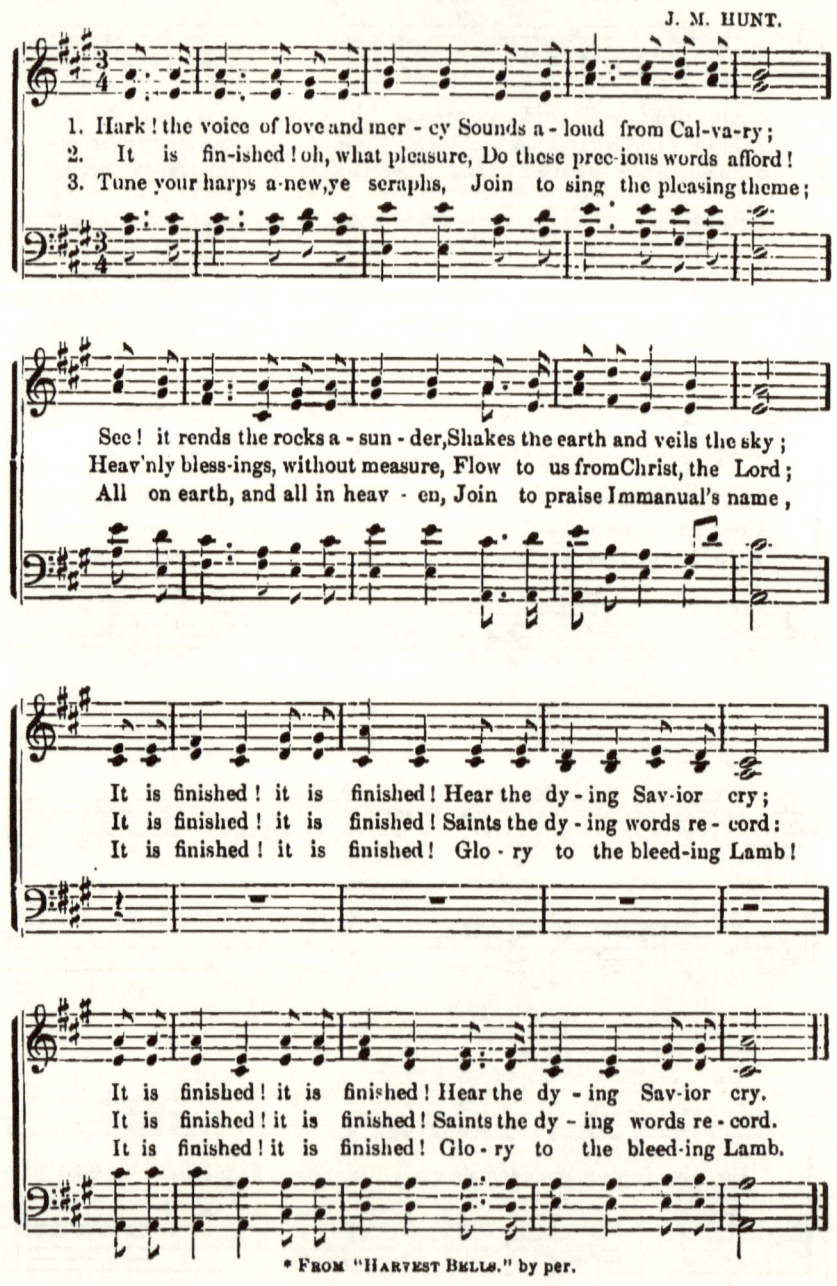

SAILING INTO PORT.

L. B. SHOOK.

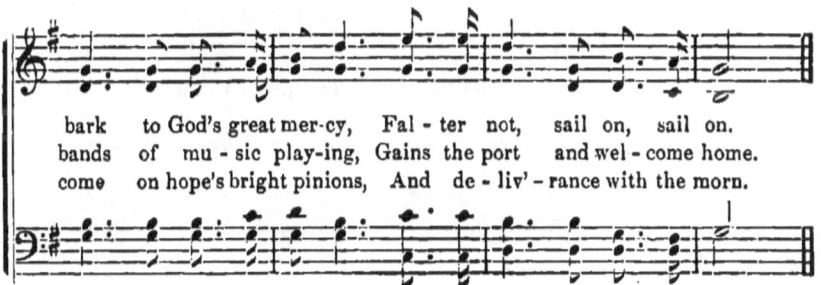

1. Sail - or, tho' the darkness gathers, Tho' the wild waves surge and moan, Trust thy bark to God's great mer-cy, Fal - ter not, sail on, sail on.
2. Sailor, tho' with streamers flying, Yonder proud ship mounts the foam, And with bands of mu - sic play-ing, Gains the port and wel - come home.
3. Sailor, tho' the light'ning flashes, Tho' thy sails be rent and torn, Peace shall come on hope's bright pinions, And de - liv' - rance with the morn.

CHORUS.

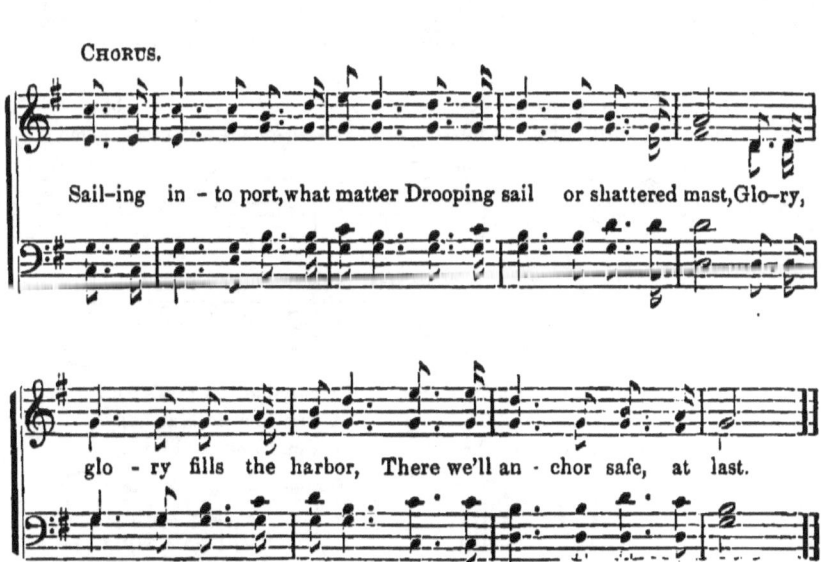

Sail-ing in - to port, what matter Drooping sail or shattered mast, Glo-ry, glo - ry fills the harbor, There we'll an - chor safe, at last.

52. THE MORNING LIGHT IS BREAKING.

S. F. SMITH.   L. B. SHOOK.

1. The morning light is breaking; The darkness dis-ap-pears; The sons of earth are wak-ing To pen-i-ten-tial tears, Each breeze that sweeps the o-cean Brings tid-ings from a-far, Of na-tions in com-mo-tion, Prepared for Zi-on's war.
2. See heath-en nations bend-ing Be-fore the God we love, And thousand hearts ascend-ing In grat-i-tude a-bove; While sin-ners, now con-fess-ing, The gos-pel call o-bey, And seek a Sav-ior's bless-ing, A na-tion in a day.
3. Blest riv-er of Sal-va-tion, Pur-sue thy on-ward way; Flow thou to ev-ery na-tion, Nor in thy rich-ness stay; Stay not till all the low-ly Tri-um-phant reach their home; Stay not till all the ho-ly Proclaim, "The Lord is come."

54. WHAT CAN CHILDREN DO?

ELIZA M. SHERMAN. J. G. BURDICK.

1. We can tell the sweet old sto-ry, We can sing of Christ's dear love,
2. We can give a cup of wa-ter, In our loving Savior's name,
3. Tho' we are but lit-tle children, We can sing and we can pray,
4. Je-sus says the fragrant lil-ies "Toil not, neither do they spin,"

How He came to lit-tle children, From His shining home above.
We can say tho' weak and sin-ful, Je-sus loves you just the same.
We can love the blessed Je-sus, Walk beside him ev-'ry day.
But, they live in His dear presence, Giving all they have to Him.

CHORUS.

We can tell, tell the sto-ry, We can
We can tell the sto-ry, We can tell the sto-ry,

sing of His love, How the King, King of
We can tell His love, we can tell His love, How the King of glo-ry,

glo-ry, Came from heav'n from, heav'n a-bove, a-bove.
How the King of glory, Came from heav'n above, from heav'n a-bove.

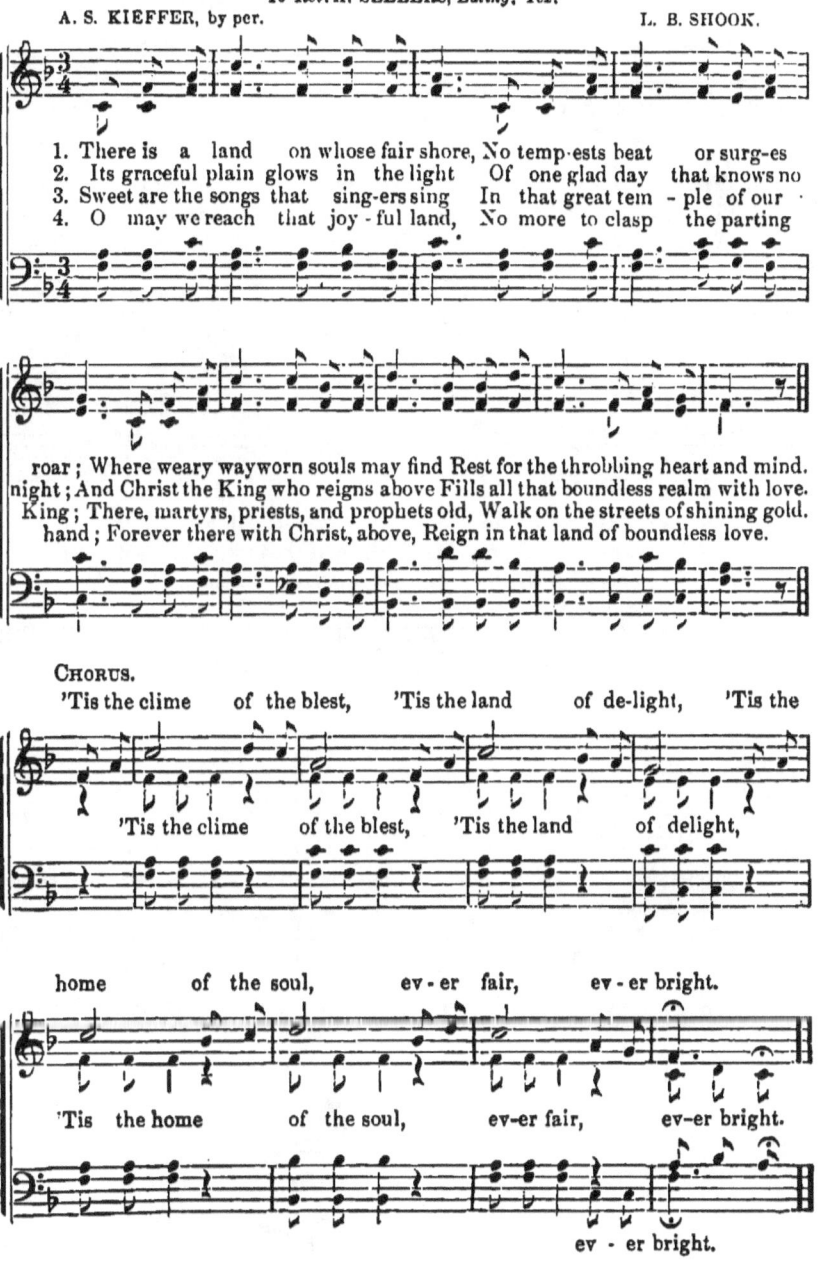

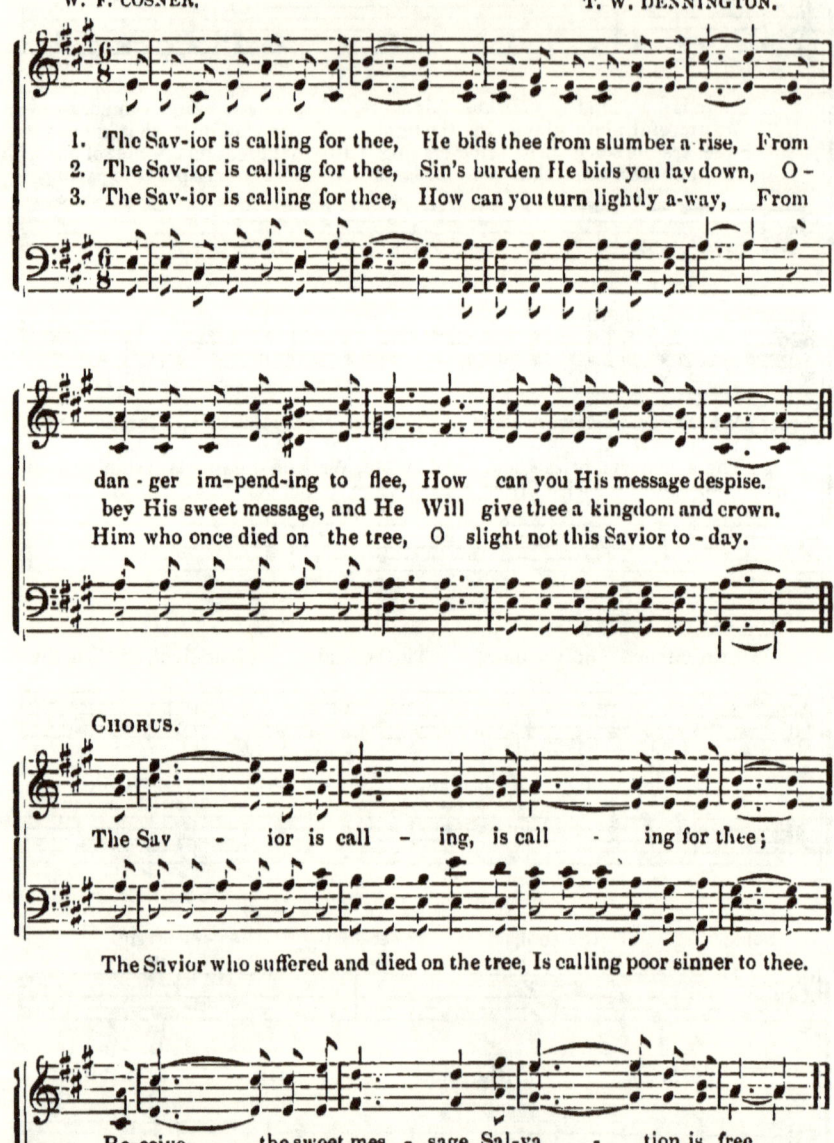

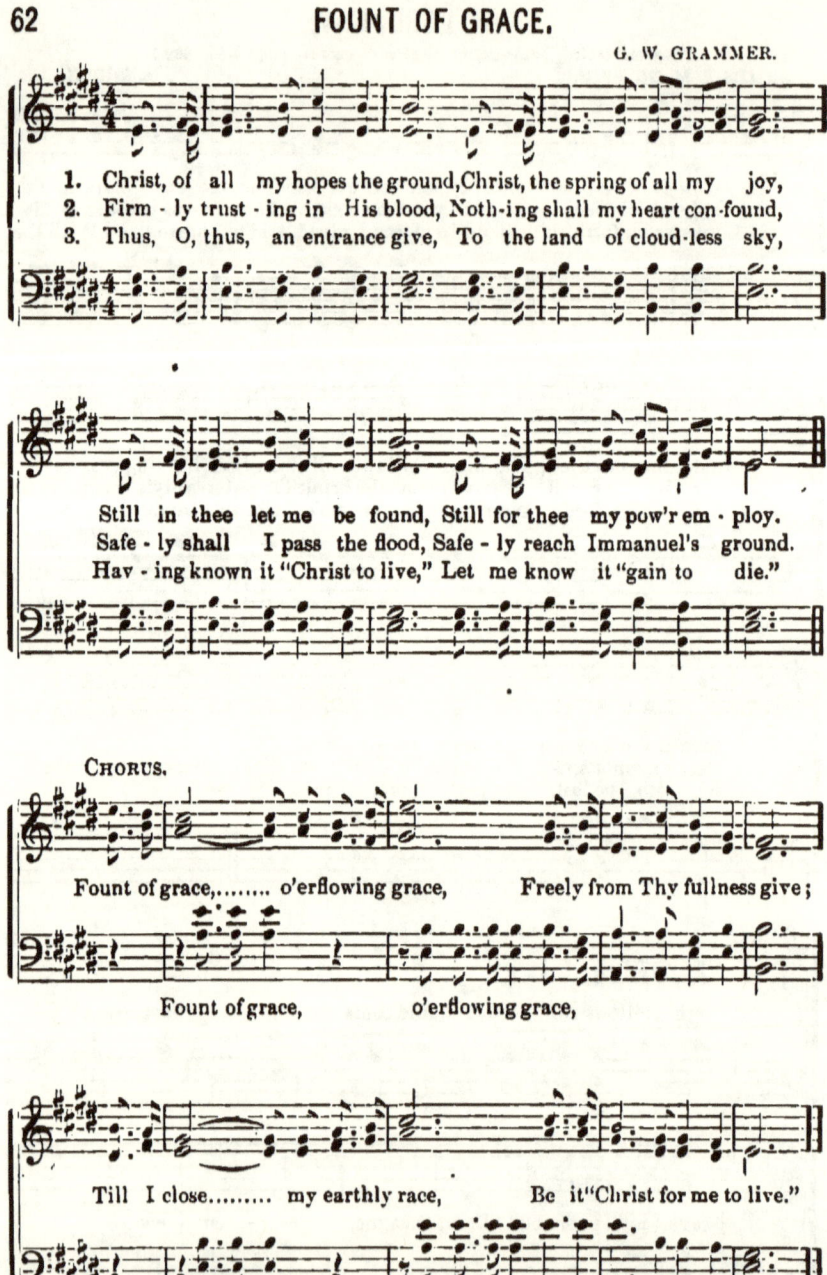

I NOW BELIEVE.

JOHN NEWTON.   CHAS. EDW. POLLOCK, by per.

1. How sweet the name of Je-sus sounds in a be-liev-er's ear! It
2. It makes the wounded spirit whole, And calms the troubled breast; 'Tis
3. Weak is the ef-fort of my heart, And cold my warmest tho't; But
4. Till then I would thy love proclaim, With ev-ery feel-ing breath; And

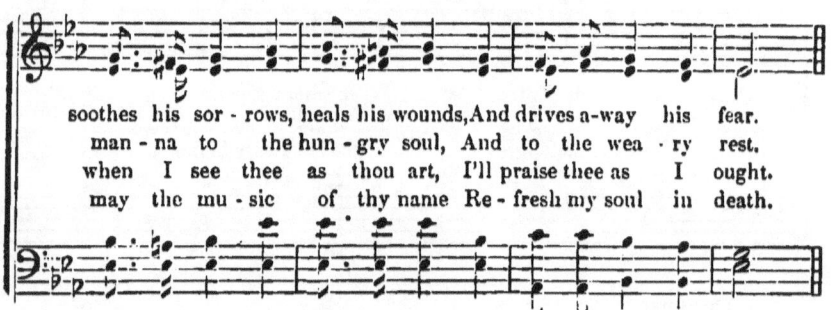

soothes his sor-rows, heals his wounds, And drives a-way his fear.
man-na to the hun-gry soul, And to the wea-ry rest.
when I see thee as thou art, I'll praise thee as I ought.
may the mu-sic of thy name Re-fresh my soul in death.

CHORUS.

I do believe, I now believe, That Jesus died for me, And

thro' His blood, His precious blood, I shall from sin be free.

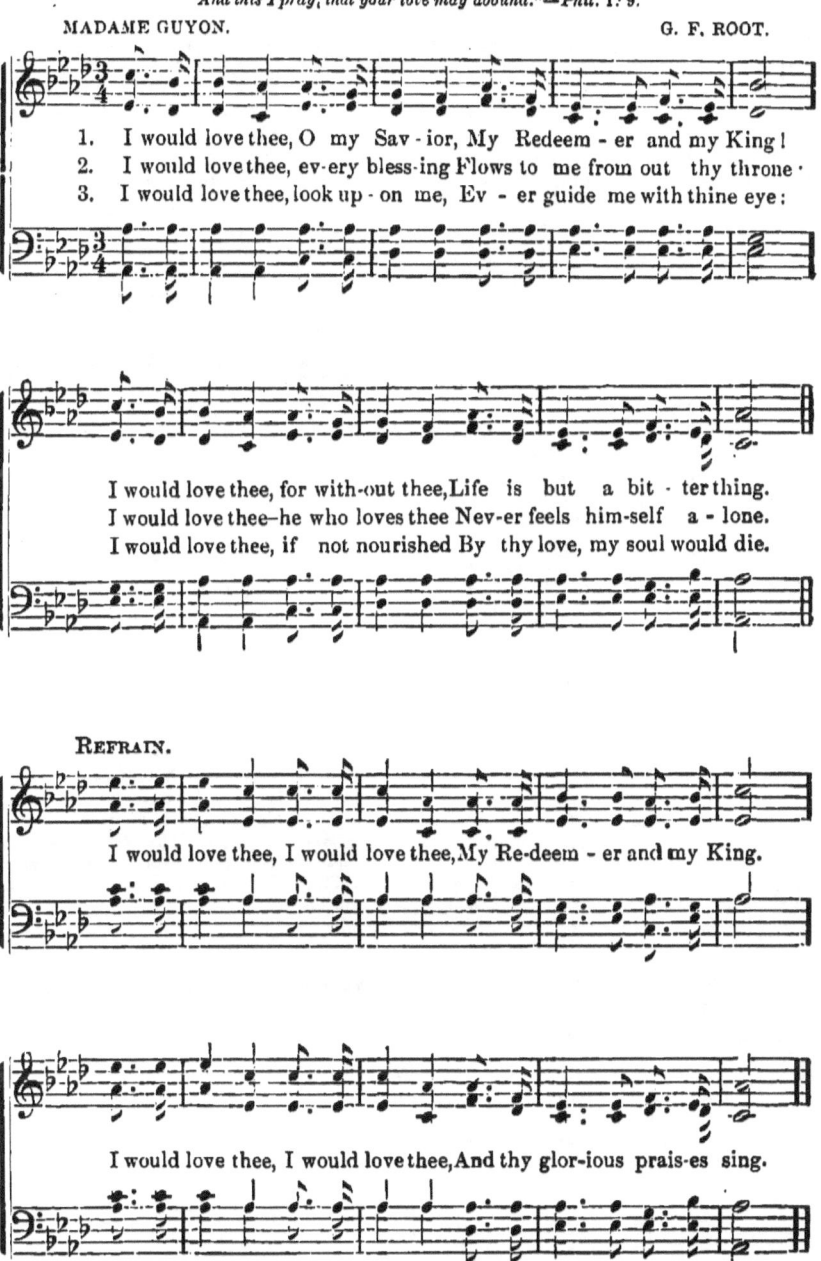

PRECIOUS THINGS.

REV. FRANK POLLOCK
CHAS. EDW. POLLOCK

1. Prec-ious Je-sus, Son of glo-ry, Light-ing up e-ter-nal skies,...... Cheer-ing saints thro' storm-y tri-als, Till they reach the bless-ed prize,...... "Prec-ious Je-sus," sing, earth's pil-grims, With the stream of death be-fore,...... "Prec-ious
2. Prec-ious faith that cleaves to Je-sus, In the dark-ness and the light,........ Prec-ious faith that in af-flic-tion, Sweet-er grows the hu-man night,...... Prec-ious faith that draw-eth cour-age, When one's strength is near-ly gone,...... Which in
3. Prec-ious tri-als, when we bear them In the pa-tience of our Lord,...... Prec-ious tri-als, how they teach us To o-bey His ho-ly word,...... Ah! to us how much more prec-ious, Than the pure-est shin-ing gold,...... When we
4. Prec-ious death, that frees the christian From earth's trouble and its sin,.......... Prec-ious death, that o-pens heav-en Wide to let the pil-grim in,........ An-gels pay a-dor-ing won-der, While weak mor-tals start and shrink,... Ah! may
5. Prec-ious light that shines in heav-en, Coming from the great white throne,...... Flood-ing man-sions with its glo-ry, Gleaming from each prec-ious stone,...... Spark-ling from the crys-tal riv-er, On whose banks the saints have trod,...... Saints who'll

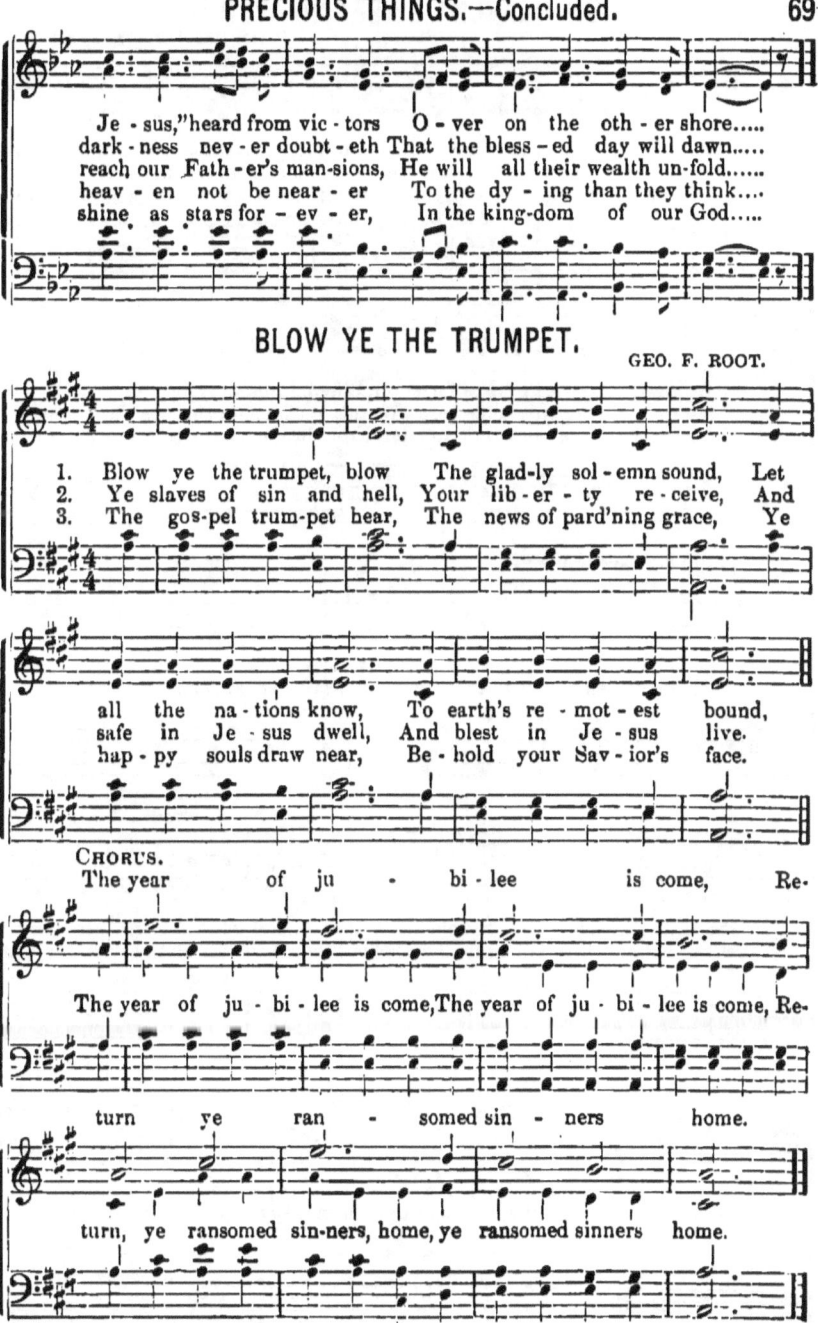

OH HEAVEN! SWEET HEAVEN!

JNO. M.
JOHN McPHERSON, by per.

1. Oh, soon we shall cross o'er the river, Our feet press those streets of pure gold;
2. Here troubles and trials be-set us, And there is no rest night or day;
3. Oh, may we soon meet far up yonder, Where trials and troubles ne'er come;

We'll sing God's sweet praises for ev-er, When Jesus' dear face we behold.
And great disappointments here fret us, We long for that rest far a-way.
Oh, sure-ly we nev-er will wan-der, From heaven, our sweet, precious home!

CHORUS.

Oh, heav - - - en, sweet heav - - en! when
Oh, heav - en sweet heav - en, Oh, heav - en, sweet heav - en! When

shall............ we behold thee, And bask............ in thy
shall we behold thee, When shall we behold thee, And bask in thy sunshine, Yes,

Repeat pp ad lib.

sun - shine e'er hap - - py to be?............
bask in thy sunshine, e'er hap-py, so hap-py, yes, hap-py to be?
 to be?

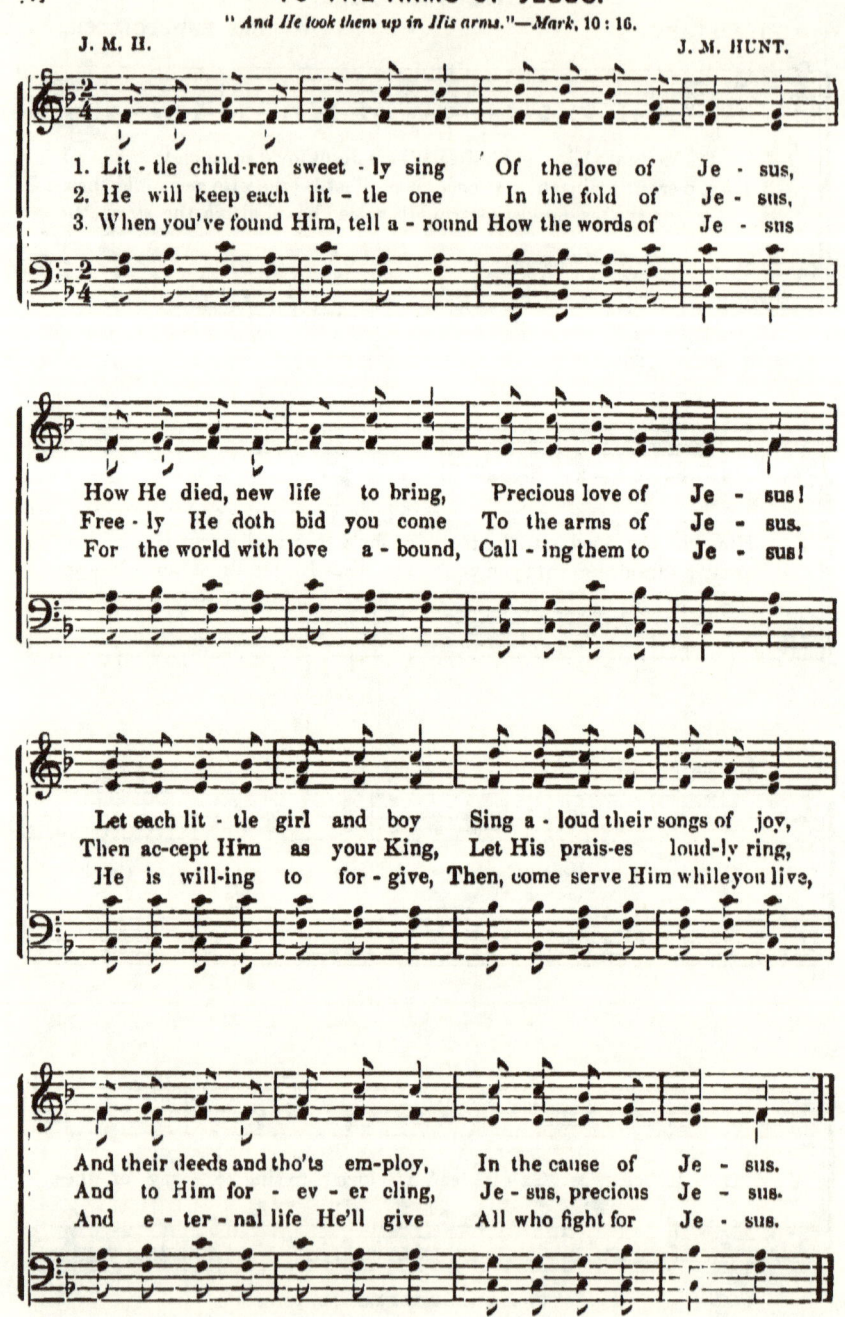

MERRY CHRISTMAS.*

Words and Music by J. R. MURRAY

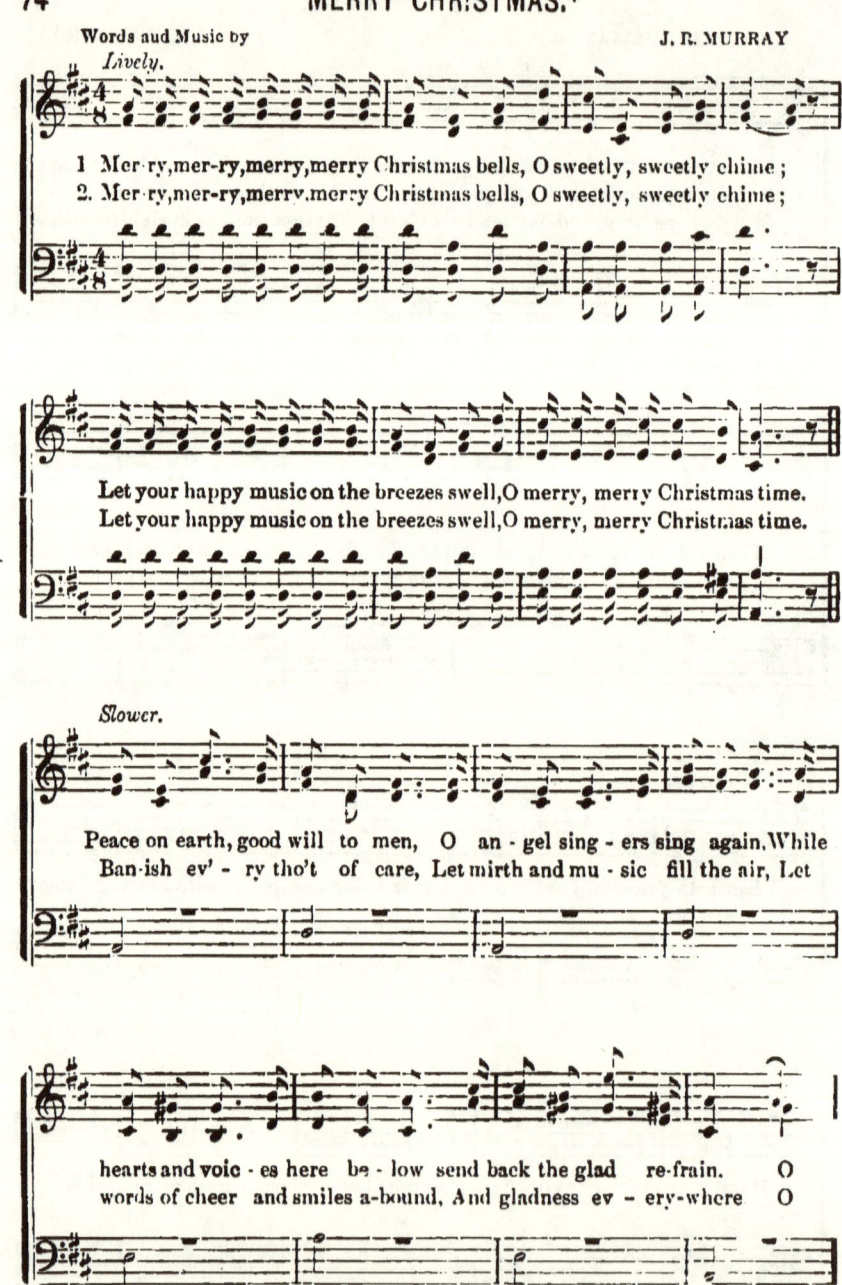

1. Mer-ry, mer-ry, merry, merry Christmas bells, O sweetly, sweetly chime;
2. Mer-ry, mer-ry, merry, merry Christmas bells, O sweetly, sweetly chime;

Let your happy music on the breezes swell, O merry, merry Christmas time.
Let your happy music on the breezes swell, O merry, merry Christmas time.

Peace on earth, good will to men, O an-gel sing-ers sing again, While
Ban-ish ev'-ry tho't of care, Let mirth and mu-sic fill the air, Let

hearts and voic-es here be-low send back the glad re-frain. O
words of cheer and smiles a-bound, And gladness ev-ery-where O

* From "PURE DIAMONDS, by per.

MERRY CHRISTMAS.—Concluded.

mer-ry, mer-ry, merry, merry Christmas bells, O sweetly, sweetly chime;
mer-ry, mer-ry, merry, merry Christmas bells, O sweetly, sweetly chime;

Let your happy music on the breezes swell, O merry, merry Christmas time.
Let your happy music on the breezes swell, O merry, merry Christmas time.

WE'RE GOING HOME.

ALLIE L. SMITH.   MISS ALLIE L. SMITH.

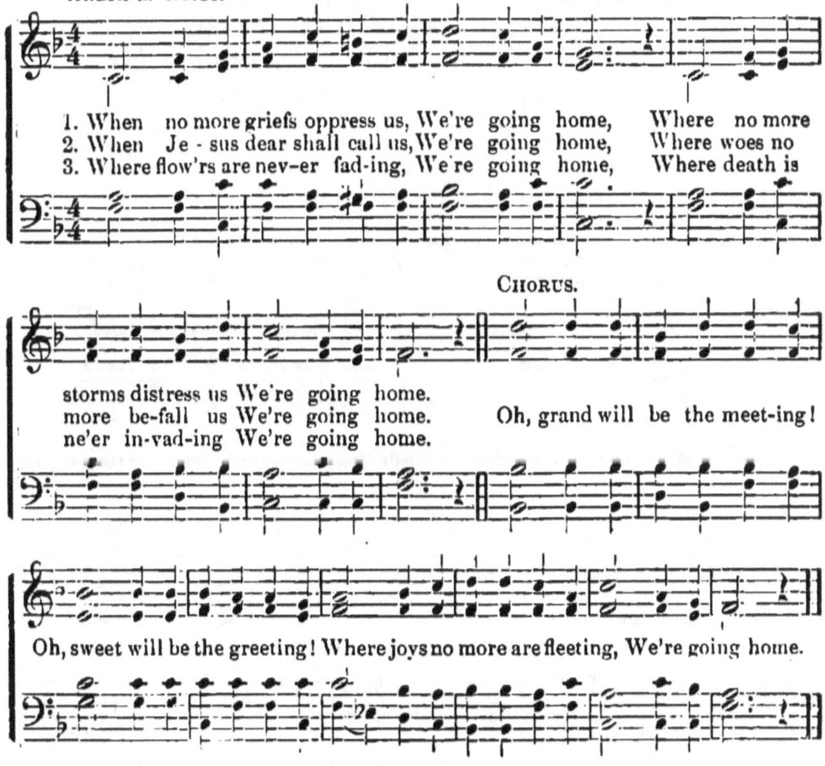

1. When no more griefs oppress us, We're going home, Where no more storms distress us We're going home.
2. When Je-sus dear shall call us, We're going home, Where woes no more be-fall us We're going home.
3. Where flow'rs are nev-er fad-ing, We're going home, Where death is ne'er in-vad-ing We're going home.

CHORUS.

Oh, grand will be the meeting! Oh, sweet will be the greeting! Where joys no more are fleeting, We're going home.

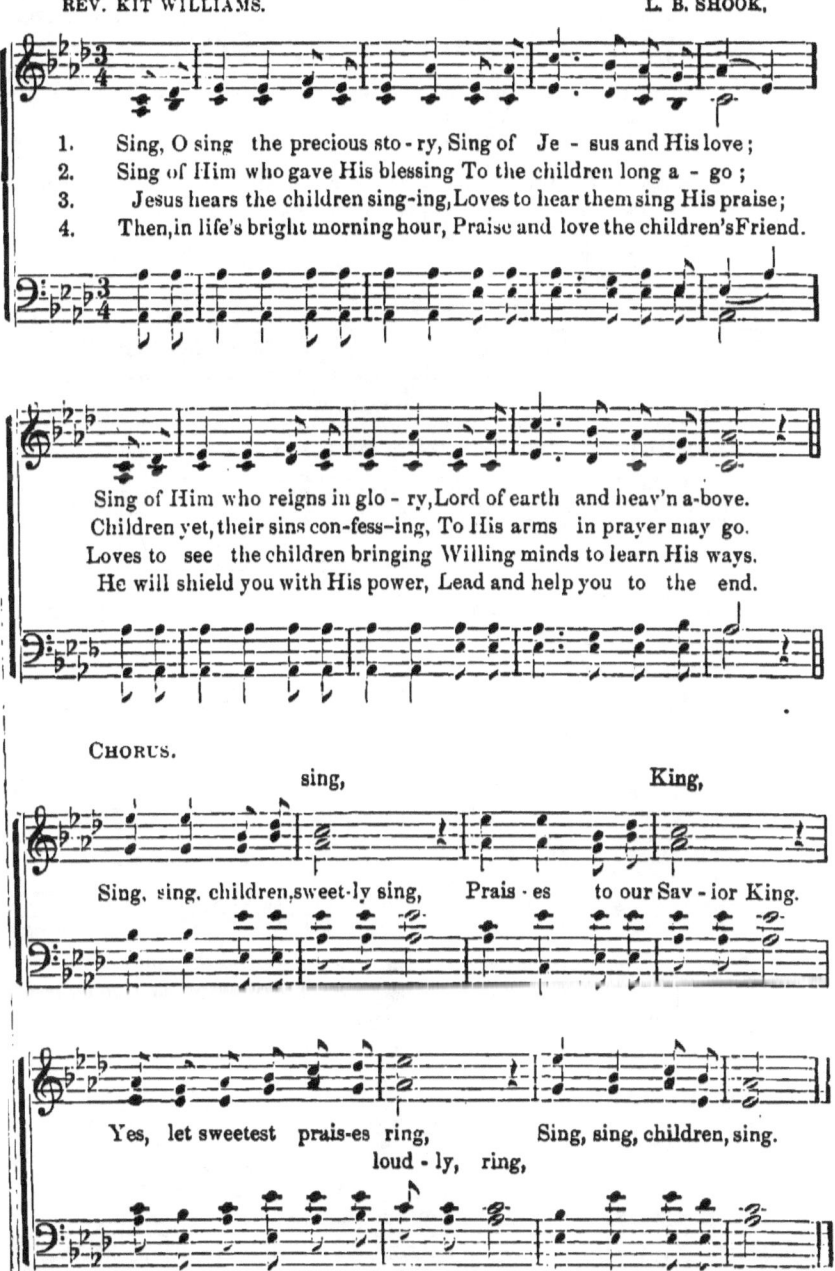

THE SUNDAY SCHOOL ARMY.

To the Sunday Schools of Luling, Texas. L. B. SHOOK.

1. The Sunday school army has gath-ered once more, Its numbers are greater than
2. We fight a-gainst e-vil, and bat-tle with wrong, Our sword is the Bible, both
3. In the midst of our con-flicts, we'll think of the Lord, Who died on the cross and
4. To Je-sus, our cap-tain, ho-san-nas we raise, And join with our teachers in

ev-er be-fore, Its banners are spread and shall never be furled, Till the
trust-y and strong, Our watchword is prayer and our faith is our shield. And [from
death was restored, To save us from sin and to give us a place With the
singing His praise, His soldiers we are, and His soldiers we'll be, Till we

CHORUS.

Prince of sal-va-tion has conquered the world.
nev-er, no, nev-er to foes will we yield.   Sing - ing,
an-gels who al-ways behold His bright face.
lay down our ar-mor and death sets us free.   Sing on our way,

Sing - ing for the army is on its bright way, March - ing,

sing on our way,   Marching a-long,

march - ing to the beau-ti-ful man-sions of day.

march-ing a-long.

THE GLAD TO-MORROW.

"Weeping may endure for the night, but joy cometh in the morning."—Psa. 30 : 5.

MRS. T. M. GRIFFIN. J. M. HUNT.

1. Tho' day hides be-yond the mountain, Leav-ing darkness deep as night;
2. Gloom-y clouds have sil-ver lin-ing, Tho' we see but dim-ly thro';
3. Prom-ise like the wings of morning, Fans a-way each trembling fear;
4. Cease thy sighing and thy sor-row, Let sweet faith her joy im-part;

Morn-ing sun will touch the fountain, With his beams of gold-en light.
Stars are in the mid night shining, Flow'rets bloom beneath the dew.
Faith a-wak'ning in the dawning, Sees the glad to-mor-row near.
Then will all be well to-mor-row, For the wounded, brok-en heart.

CHORUS.

O! the sweet, the glad to-morrow, That will dawn be-yond this vale;

O! the glorious, bright to-morrow, When the saints with Christ shall dwell.

CHILDREN'S HOSANNAS.

L. B. SHOOK.

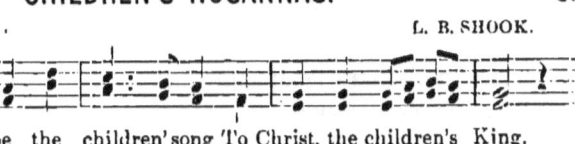
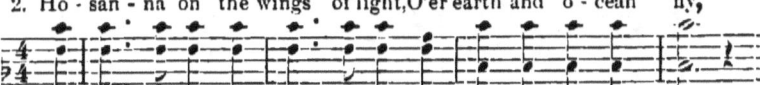

1. Ho-san-na be the children's song To Christ, the children's King.
2. Ho-san-na on the wings of light, O'er earth and o-cean fly,

His praise to whom our souls be-long, Let all the child-ren sing;
Till morn to eve, and noon to night, And heav'n to earth re-ply.

From lit-tle ones to Je-sus bro't, Ho-san-na now be heard;
Ho-san-na, then our song shall be; Ho-san-na to our King;

Let lit-tle child-ren, now, be taught, To sing that love-ly word.
This is the children's ju-bi-lee, Let all the child-ren sing.

OVER THE BEAUTIFUL HILLS.*

LINA H. BARTON. J. B. HERBERT.

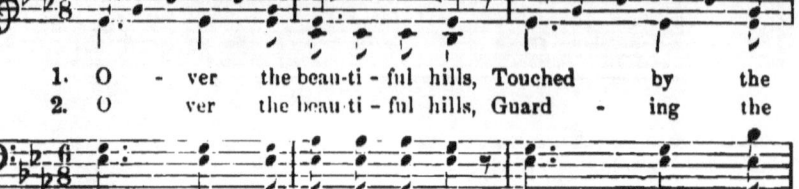

1. O-ver the beautiful hills,............ Touched by the fin-ger of
2. O-ver the beautiful hills,............ Guard-ing the gates of the

God,............
east,............

fin-ger of God, Comes the first ray of wak-en-ing day, The
gates of the east, Je-sus will come, our Light and our Sun, A

mes-sen-ger of our God........ O-ver the brighten-ing
con-quer-or, bring-ing peace....... The mountains shall tremble with

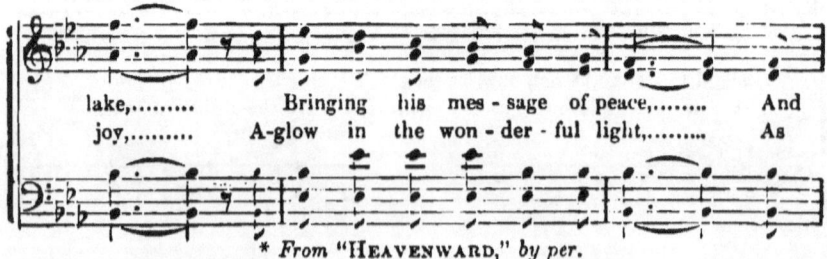

lake,......... Bringing his mes-sage of peace,......... And
joy,......... A-glow in the won-der-ful light,......... As

*From "HEAVENWARD," by per.

OVER THE BEAUTIFUL HILLS.—Concluded.

o-ver the beautiful pur-ple hills Com-eth the sun in the east......
o-ver the beautiful pur-ple hills Com-eth the glo-ry of Christ......

CHORUS.

Hail! all hail!...... the beau-ti-ful day! Glo-ri-a ti-bi

Dom - i - ne! * Hail! all hail! the

beau-ti-ful day! Glo-ri-a ti-bi Dom - i - ne!......

* Glory be to thee, O God! (Glo-ri-a tib-be Dom-e-nay.)

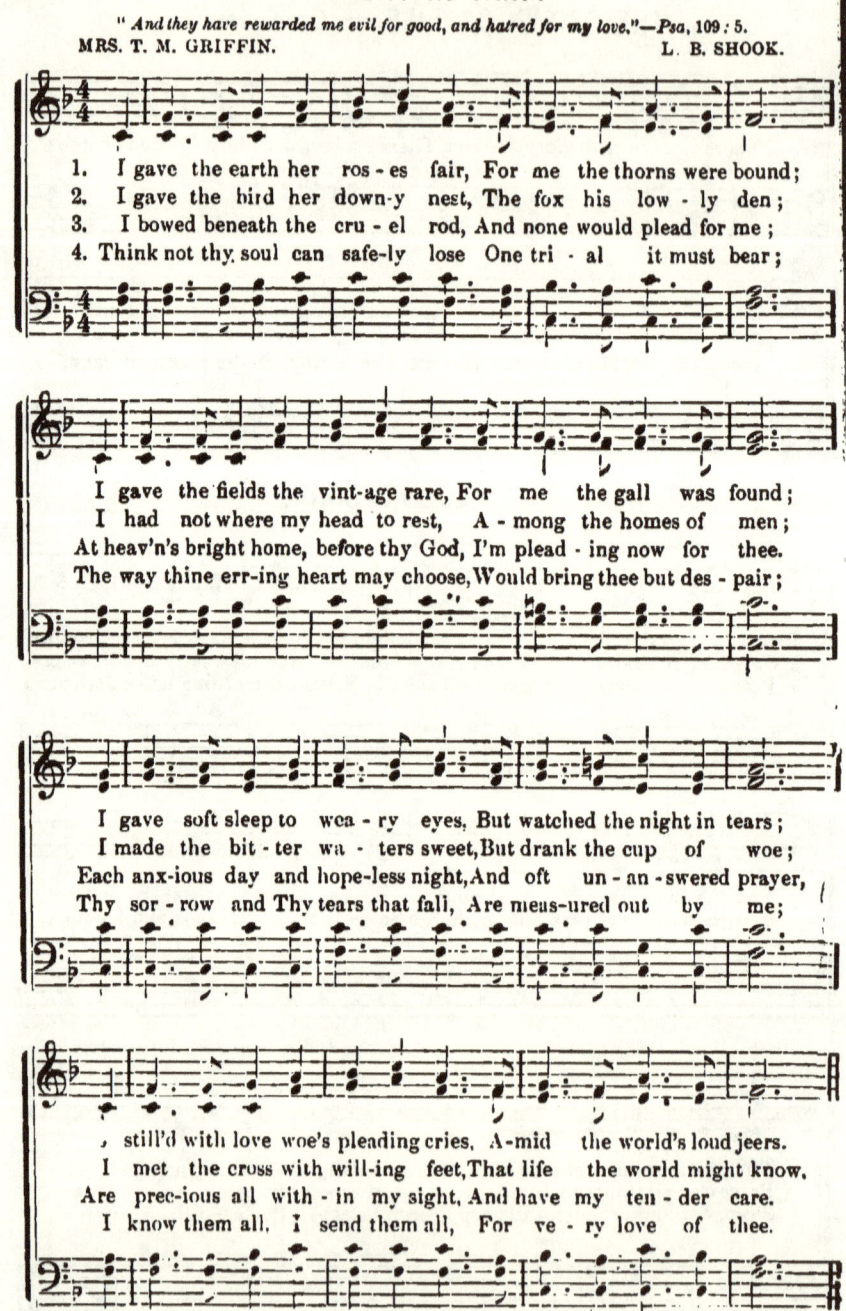

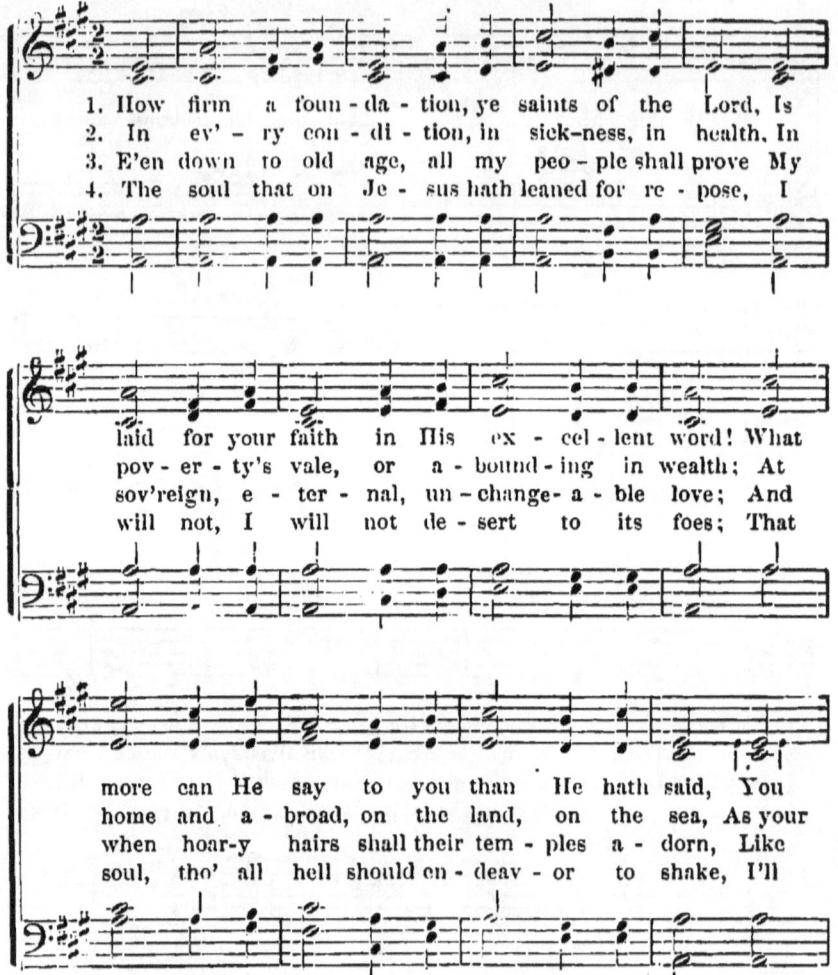

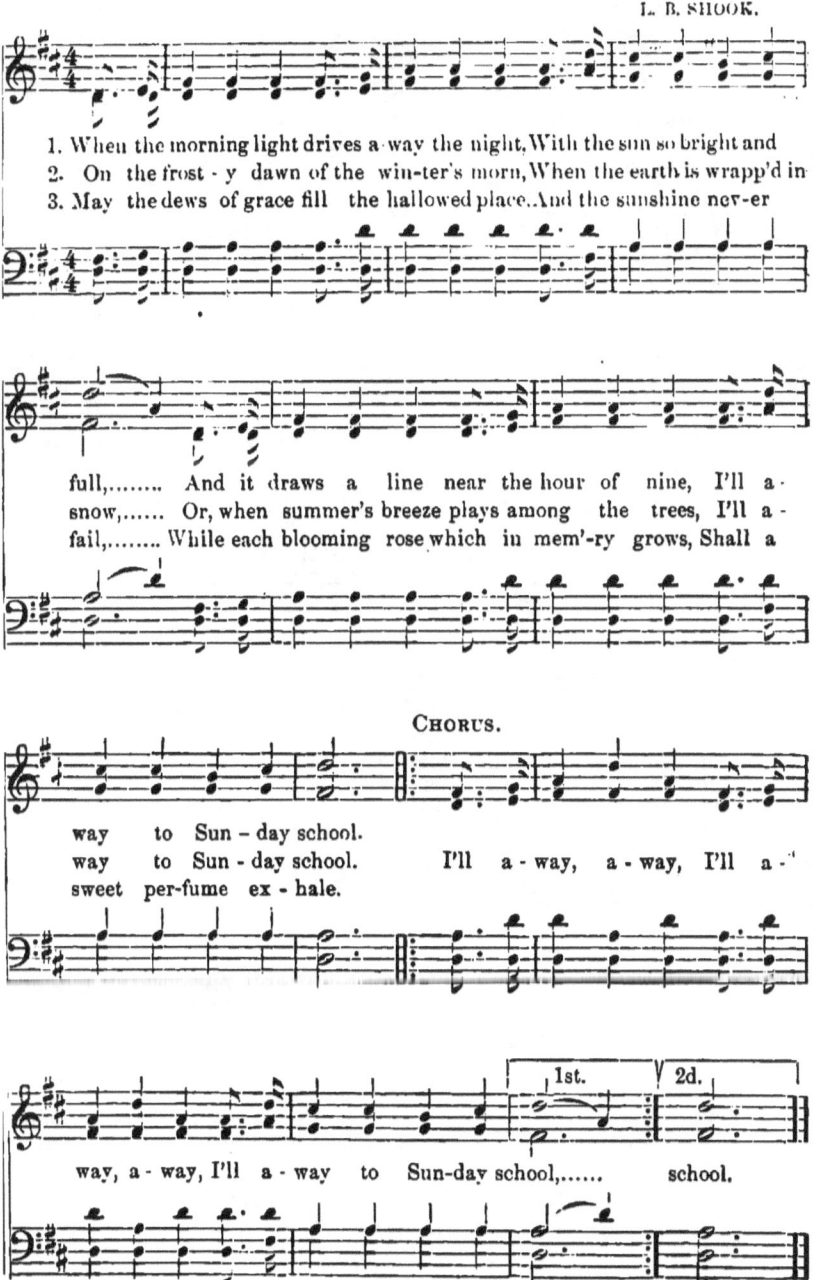

GO TELL THE JOYFUL STORY.—Concluded.

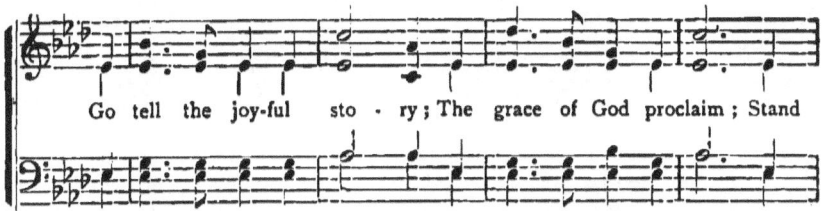

Go tell the joy-ful sto - ry; The grace of God proclaim; Stand

up, stand up, for Je - sus, Stand trust-ing in His name.

BOONE.

Arranged from an air heard years ago.

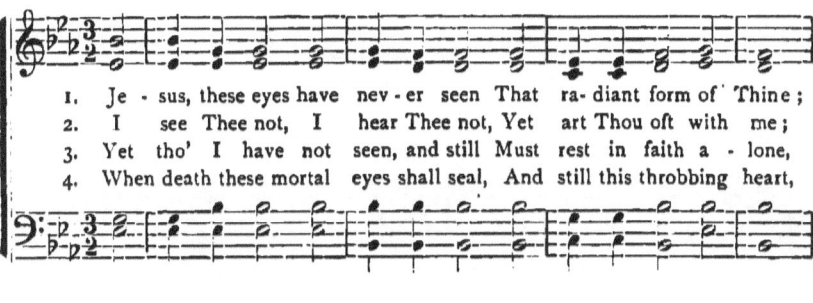

1. Je - sus, these eyes have nev - er seen That ra - diant form of Thine;
2. I see Thee not, I hear Thee not, Yet art Thou oft with me;
3. Yet tho' I have not seen, and still Must rest in faith a - lone,
4. When death these mortal eyes shall seal, And still this throbbing heart,

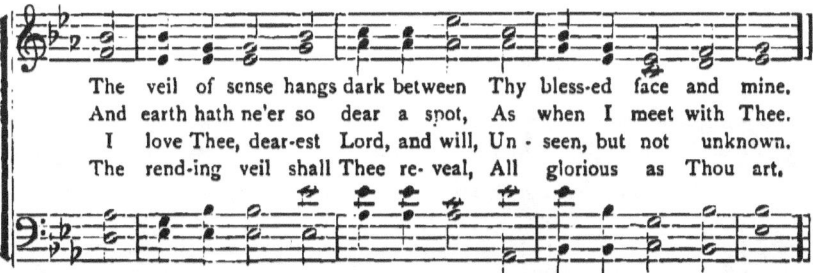

The veil of sense hangs dark between Thy bless-ed face and mine.
And earth hath ne'er so dear a spot, As when I meet with Thee.
I love Thee, dear-est Lord, and will, Un - seen, but not unknown.
The rend-ing veil shall Thee re - veal, All glorious as Thou art.

MALONE.

To Jas. M. Malone, Steeleville, Ill.

L. B. SHOOK.

1. He that go-eth forth with weeping, Bearing precious seed in love,
Nev-er tir-ing, nev-er sleeping, Find-eth mer-cy from a-bove:
Soft des-cend the dews of hea-ven, Bright the rays cel-es-tial shine;
Pre-cious fruits will thus be giv-en, Through an in-fluence all di-vine.

2. Sow thy seed, be nev-er wea-ry, Let no fears thy soul an-noy,
Be the pros-pect ne'er so drea-ry, Thou shalt reap the fruits of joy.
Lo! the scene of ver-dure brightening! See the ris-ing grain ap-pear;
Look a-gain! the fields are whitening, For the har-vest time is near.

THE GOLDEN CITY.

L. B. SHOOK.

1. We seek a gold-en cit-y, The cit-y of our King; And as we jour-ney thith-er We joy-ful-ly will sing.
2. There life's pure crys-tal riv-er E-ter-nal-ly shall flow, While leaves to heal the na-tions, Close by its wa-ters grow.
3. But through that gold-en cit-y Our loud-est praise shall ring, When we be-hold our Sav-ior, Our Pro-phet, Priest and King.

CHORUS.

Come, then, children, let us sweet-ly sing;

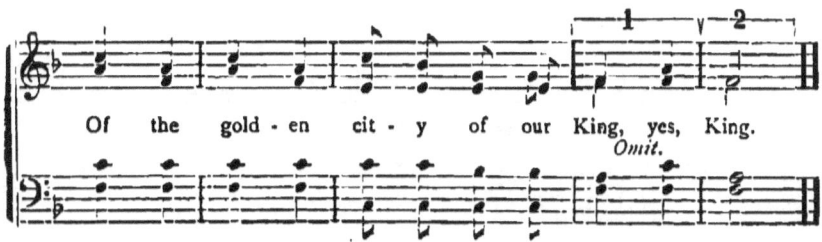

Of the gold-en cit-y of our King, yes, King.
Omit.

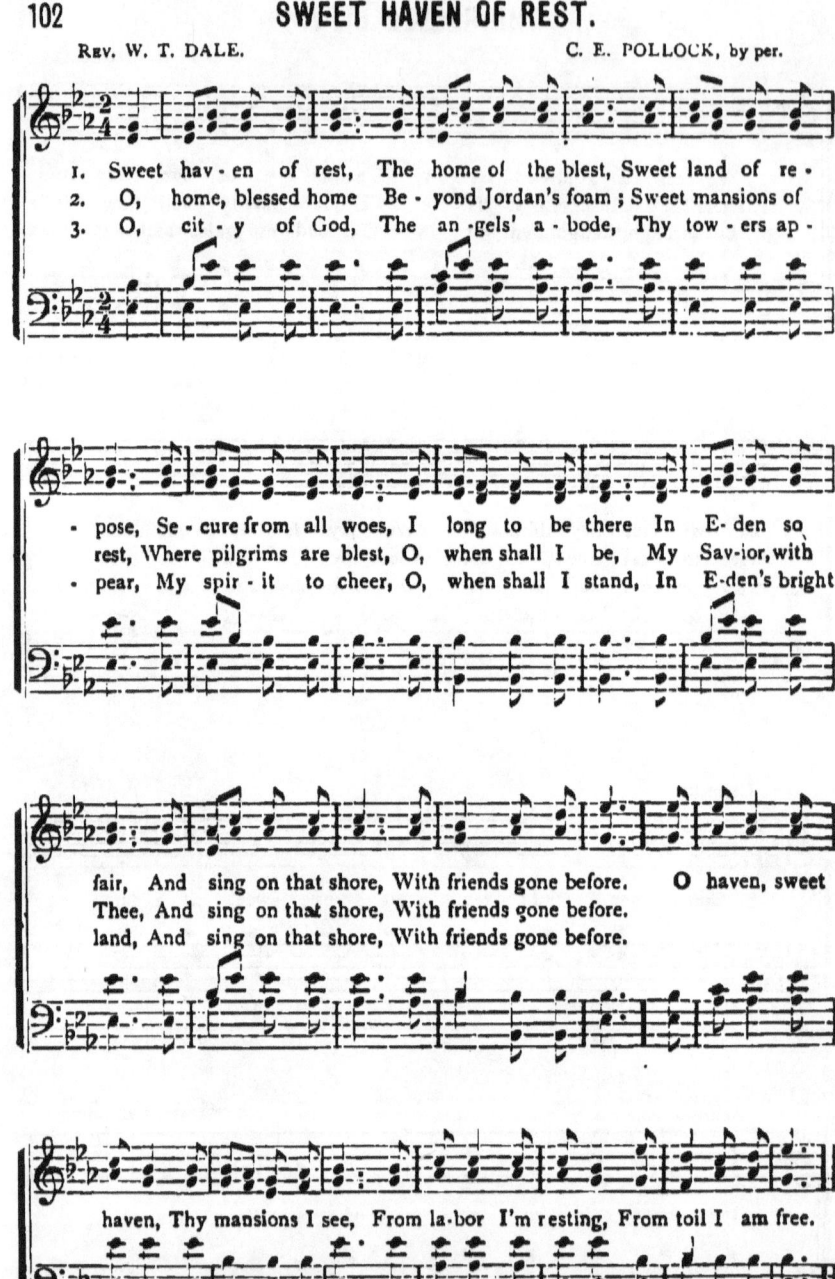

FLOW ON.

FRANK L. HUNT.

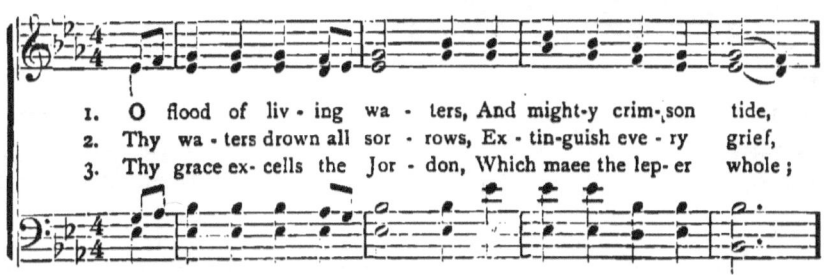

1. O flood of liv-ing wa-ters, And might-y crim-son tide,
2. Thy wa-ters drown all sor-rows, Ex-tin-guish eve-ry grief,
3. Thy grace ex-cells the Jor-don, Which maee the lep-er whole;

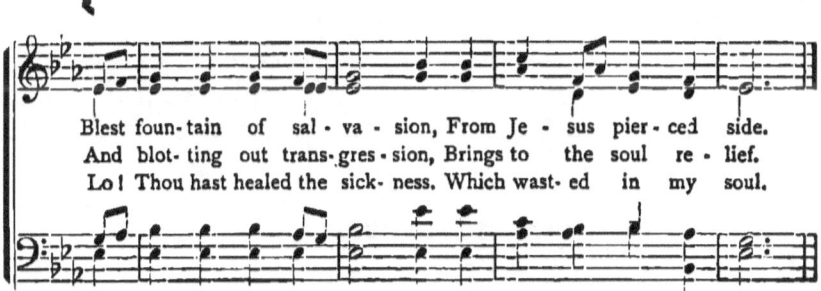

Blest foun-tain of sal-va-sion, From Je-sus pier-ced side.
And blot-ting out trans-gres-sion, Brings to the soul re-lief.
Lo! Thou hast healed the sick-ness, Which wast-ed in my soul.

CHORUS.

Flow on, flow on, O, sa-cred stream, flow on,
Flow on, flow on, flow on,

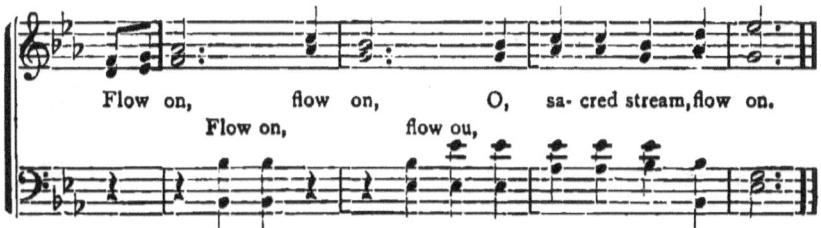

Flow on, flow on, O, sa-cred stream, flow on.
Flow on, flow ou,

SAINTS' HOME.

107

W. E. PENN. L. B. SHOOK.

COME TO OUR FATHER'S HOUSE.

ALDINE S. KIEFFER, by per. L. B. SHOOK.

1. Come to our Father's house, Come, ere the day be gone;
2. Look at the wea-ry way, Look, where thy feet have trod,
3. Dark-er the path-way grows, Soon will the night come down,
4. Fly from the fields of sin, Fly for thy life to-day!

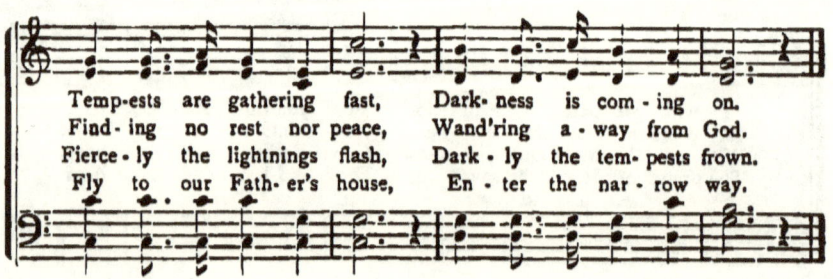

Temp-ests are gathering fast, Dark-ness is com-ing on.
Find-ing no rest nor peace, Wand'ring a-way from God.
Fierce-ly the lightnings flash, Dark-ly the tem-pests frown.
Fly to our Fath-er's house, En-ter the nar-row way.

CHORUS.

Fly, for the tempest is com-ing, Sweeping the fields of sin;

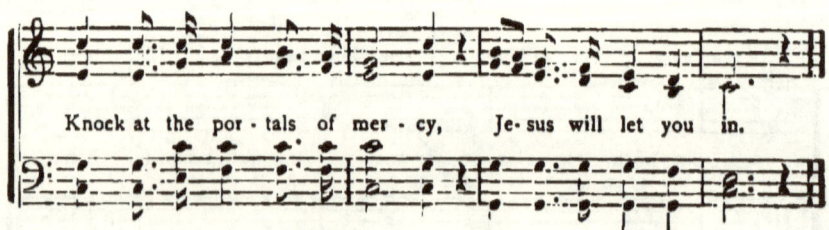

Knock at the por-tals of mer-cy, Je-sus will let you in.

THE LORD IS NEAR.

Abide in me, and I in you.—John 15: 4.

Mrs. T. M. GRIFFIN. L. B. SHOOK.
DUET.

1. In the si-lent hour of twi-light, When the days last mur-mur dies,
2. In the smil-ing race for plea-sure, When the moments swift-ly fly,
3. In the weeping night of sor-row, When the heart in an-guish lies,

In the sol-emn hush of mid-night, When the world in slumber lies,
In the bu-sy search for trea-sure, If there comes a long-ing sigh,
Try-ing vain-ly peace to bor-row, If a prayer to heaven a-rise,

Comes His gen-tle spir-it steal-ing To the soul with ten-der care,
'Tis His gen-tle spir-it steal-ing To the soul with ten-der care,
Then His gen-tle spir-it steal-ing To the soul with ten-der care,

And the "still small voice," ap-peal-ing, "A-bide in Me," the Lord is near.
'Tis His "still small voice," ap-peal-ing, "A-bide in Me," the Lord is near.
Says in "still small voice," ap-peal-ing, "A-bide in Me," the Lord is near.

REFRAIN.   dim.   ri.

"A - bide in me," The Lord is near.

I NEED THE LOVE OF JESUS—Concluded.

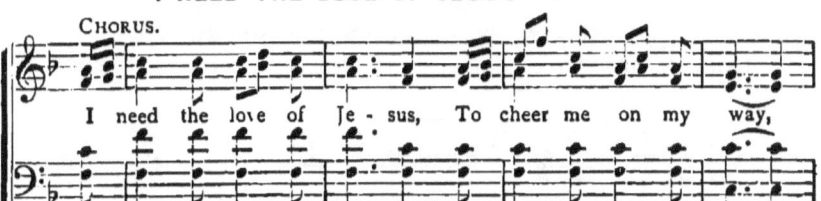

I need the love of Jesus, To cheer me on my way,

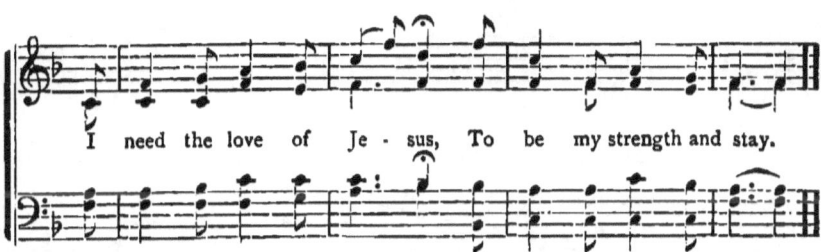

I need the love of Jesus, To be my strength and stay.

GOOD NIGHT. (Avon.)

JOHN McPHERSON. SCOTTISH.

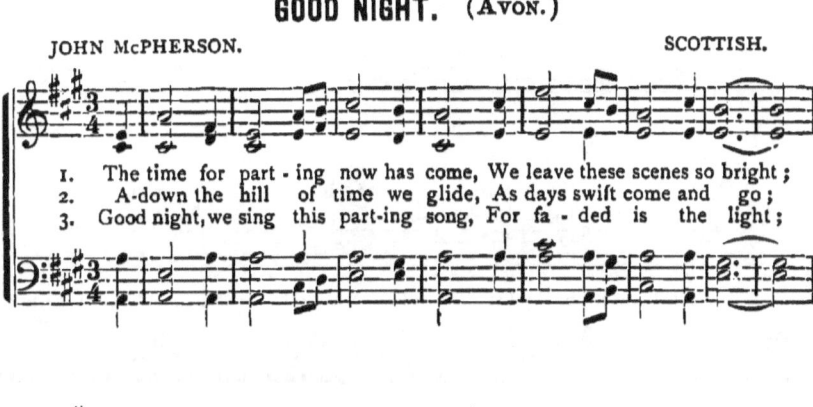

1. The time for part-ing now has come, We leave these scenes so bright;
2. A-down the hill of time we glide, As days swift come and go;
3. Good night, we sing this part-ing song, For fa-ded is the light;

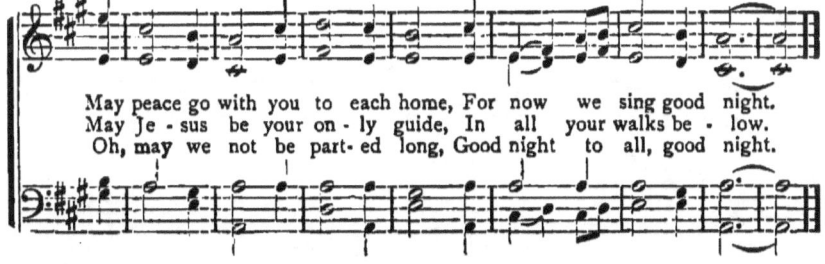

May peace go with you to each home, For now we sing good night.
May Jesus be your on-ly guide, In all your walks be-low.
Oh, may we not be part-ed long, Good night to all, good night.

THE BEAUTIFUL ROBE.

"And white robes were given unto every one of them.—Rev. 6: 11.

Mrs. T. M. GRIFFIN. L. B. SHOOK.

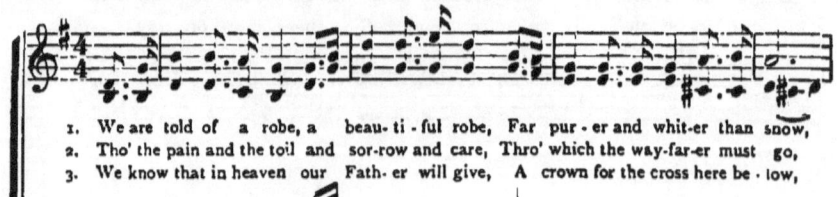

1. We are told of a robe, a beau-ti-ful robe, Far pur-er and whit-er than snow,
2. Tho' the pain and the toil and sor-row and care, Thro' which the way-far-er must go,
3. We know that in heaven our Fath-er will give, A crown for the cross here be-low,

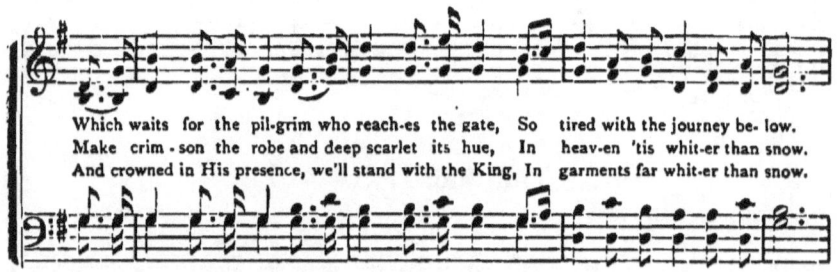

Which waits for the pil-grim who reach-es the gate, So tired with the journey be-low.
Make crim-son the robe and deep scarlet its hue, In heav-en 'tis whit-er than snow.
And crowned in His presence, we'll stand with the King, In garments far whit-er than snow.

CHORUS.

O, beau - ti-ful robe,...... far whit - er than snow,......
Beau-ti-ful robe, beautiful robe, whiter than snow, whiter than snow,

O, beau - ti-ful robe,......
Beauti-ful robe, beauti-ful robe,'Tis worth all the pain and woe.

PASS ALONG THE WATCHWORD.

CALVARY BAPTIST SUNDAY SCHOOL, SACRAMENTO, CAL.

L. B. SHOOK.

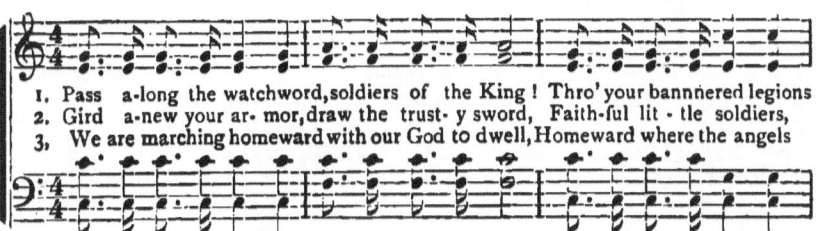

1. Pass a-long the watchword, soldiers of the King! Thro' your bannnered legions
2. Gird a-new your ar- mor, draw the trust- y sword, Faith-ful lit - tle soldiers,
3. We are marching homeward with our God to dwell, Homeward where the angels

let the war- cry ring! Pass a - long the watchword as you on-ward go,
fight-ing for the Lord; Je - sus Christ, your Captain, gives you as you go,
songs of tri-umph swell. There we'll gladly gath-er, no more out to go,

CHORUS. *f*

Vic- to- ry, yes, vic - to- ry, o - ver eve- ry foe. Pass aloug the watchword,
Vic- to- ry, yes, vic - to- ry, o - ver eve- ry foe.
Vic- to- ry, yes, vic - to- ry, ours o'er eve- ry foe.

Repeat ff.

shout it as you go, Vic - to- ry! yes, vic- to- ry! o - ver eve- ry foe.

OH, YES, I WILL COME TO THE SAVIOR.

L. B. SHOOK.

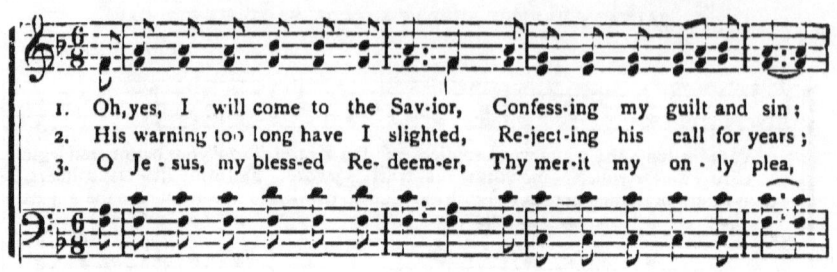

1. Oh, yes, I will come to the Sav-ior, Confess-ing my guilt and sin;
2. His warning too long have I slighted, Re-ject-ing his call for years;
3. O Je-sus, my bless-ed Re-deem-er, Thy mer-it my on-ly plea,

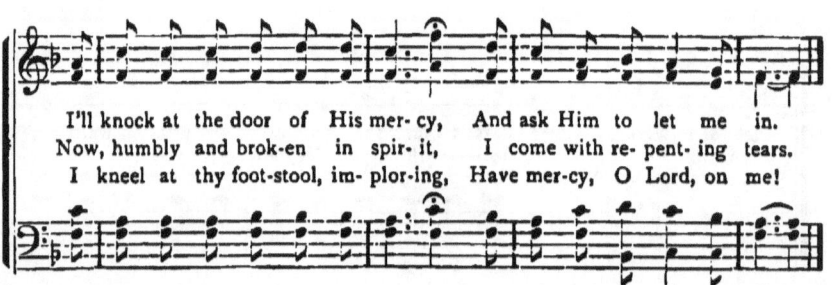

I'll knock at the door of His mer-cy, And ask Him to let me in.
Now, humbly and brok-en in spir-it, I come with re-pent-ing tears.
I kneel at thy foot-stool, im-plor-ing, Have mer-cy, O Lord, on me!

CHORUS.

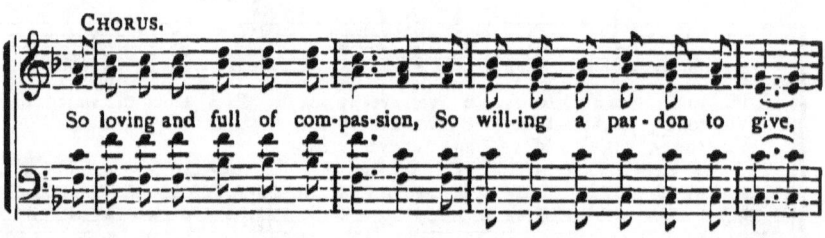

So loving and full of com-pas-sion, So will-ing a par-don to give,

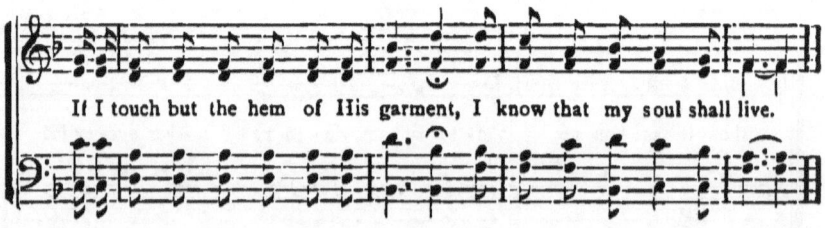

If I touch but the hem of His garment, I know that my soul shall live.

THERE IS JOY.

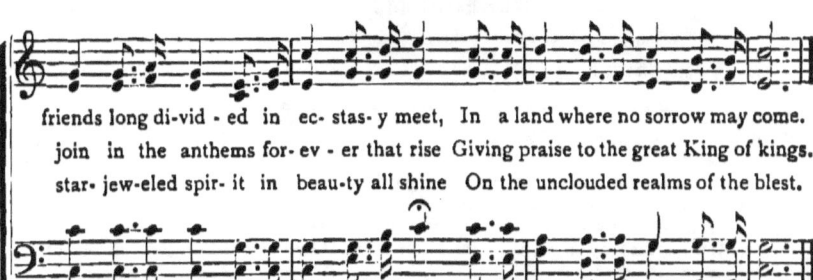

friends long di-vid-ed in ec-stas-y meet, In a land where no sorrow may come.
join in the anthems for-ev-er that rise Giving praise to the great King of kings.
star-jew-eled spir-it in beau-ty all shine On the unclouded realms of the blest.

CHORUS.

There is joy, joy, joy, There is joy, joy, joy, There is

joy in the hea-vens a-bove, There is joy, joy, joy, There is

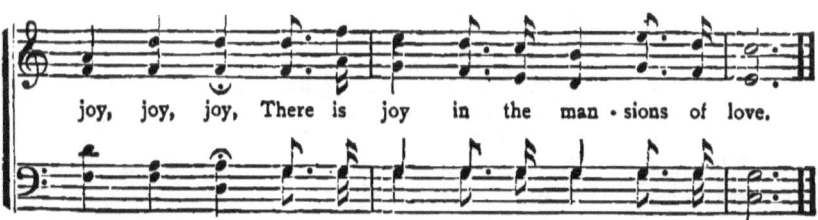

joy, joy, joy, There is joy in the man-sions of love.

118

Respectfully Inscribed to Rev. R. M. Currie, by T. M. G.

NEARING MY HOME.

"When ye shall see all these things, know that it is near."—Matt. 24: 33.

Mrs. T. M. GRIFFIN. L. B. SHOOK.

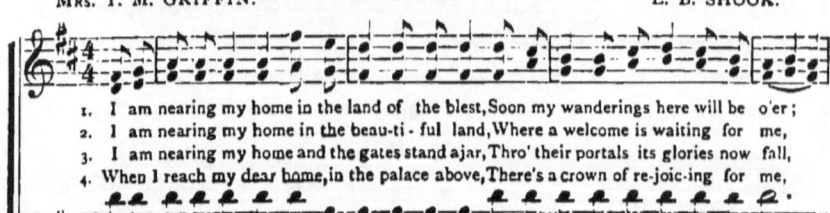

1. I am nearing my home in the land of the blest, Soon my wanderings here will be o'er;
2. I am nearing my home in the beau-ti-ful land, Where a welcome is waiting for me,
3. I am nearing my home and the gates stand ajar, Thro' their portals its glories now fall,
4. When I reach my dear home, in the palace above, There's a crown of re-joic-ing for me,

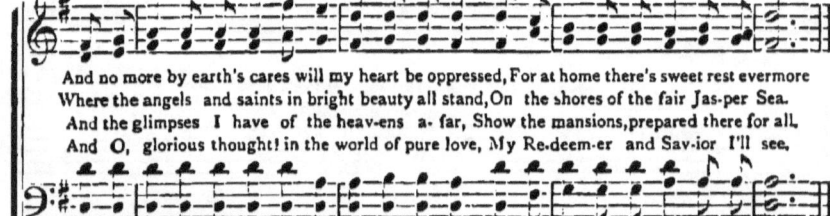

And no more by earth's cares will my heart be oppressed, For at home there's sweet rest evermore
Where the angels and saints in bright beauty all stand, On the shores of the fair Jas-per Sea.
And the glimpses I have of the heav-ens a-far, Show the mansions, prepared there for all.
And O, glorious thought! in the world of pure love, My Re-deem-er and Sav-ior I'll see.

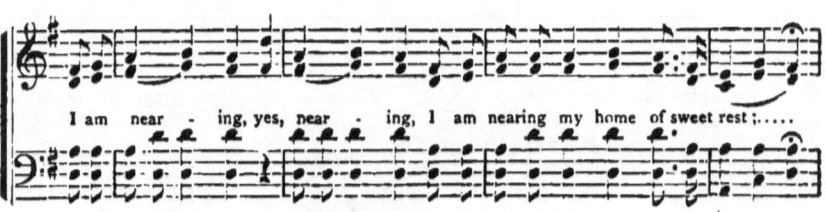

I am near - ing, yes, near - ing, I am nearing my home of sweet rest;.....
I am nearing my home, nearing my home, sweet rest;

I am near - ing, yes, near - ing,

I am nearing my home, yes, near-ing my home, I am nearing the land of the blest.

SING OF HIS LOVE.

L. B. SHOOK, Sacramento, Cal,. Feb. 5th, 1883.

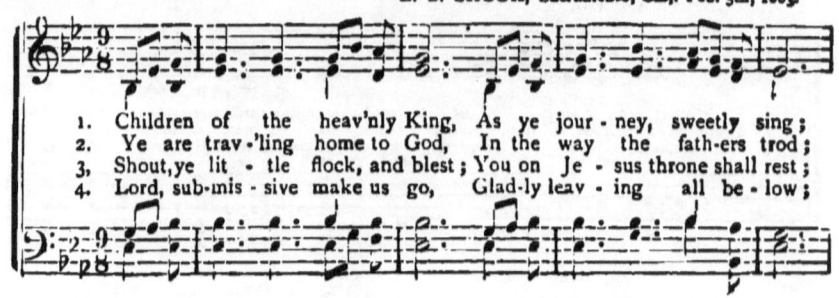

1. Children of the heav'nly King, As ye jour-ney, sweetly sing;
2. Ye are trav-'ling home to God, In the way the fath-ers trod;
3. Shout, ye lit-tle flock, and blest; You on Je-sus throne shall rest;
4. Lord, sub-mis-sive make us go, Glad-ly leav-ing all be-low;

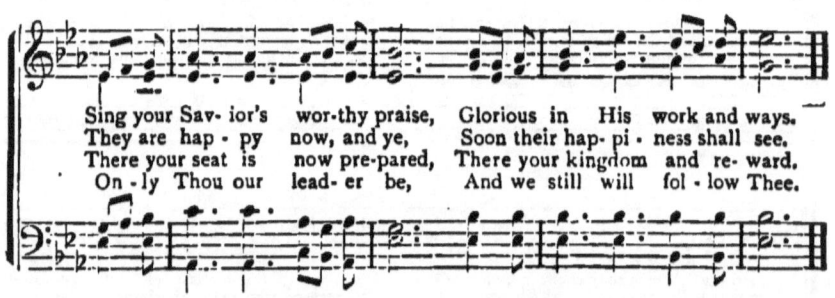

Sing your Sav-ior's wor-thy praise, Glorious in His work and ways.
They are hap-py now, and ye, Soon their hap-pi-ness shall see.
There your seat is now pre-pared, There your kingdom and re-ward.
On-ly Thou our lead-er be, And we still will fol-low Thee.

CHORUS.

Sing of His love,............ Ye angels of light,............ Car-rol His

Sing of His love, Ye an-gels of light,

praise,...... Ye seraphs so bright;........ Join in the song,............ Ye saints with de-

Carrol His praise, Ye seraphs so bright, Join in the song

SING OF HIS LOVE. Concluded.

Ye saints with delight, Praising the name of Je-sus our King.

SEEK A SAVIOR'S BLESSING.

ALLIE L. SMITH.   Miss ALLIE L. SMITH.

1. Would you have the Sav-ior near? Come, your sins con-fess-ing;
2. When your footsteps stray from God, Come, your sins con-fess-ing;

Would you have His love and cheer? Come, and seek His bless-ing.
Back-ward trace the path you've trod, Come, and seek His bless-ing.

CHORUS.

He of-fers life to-day, He is the on-ly way,

To him, bow your heart and pray, He will sure-ly bless you.

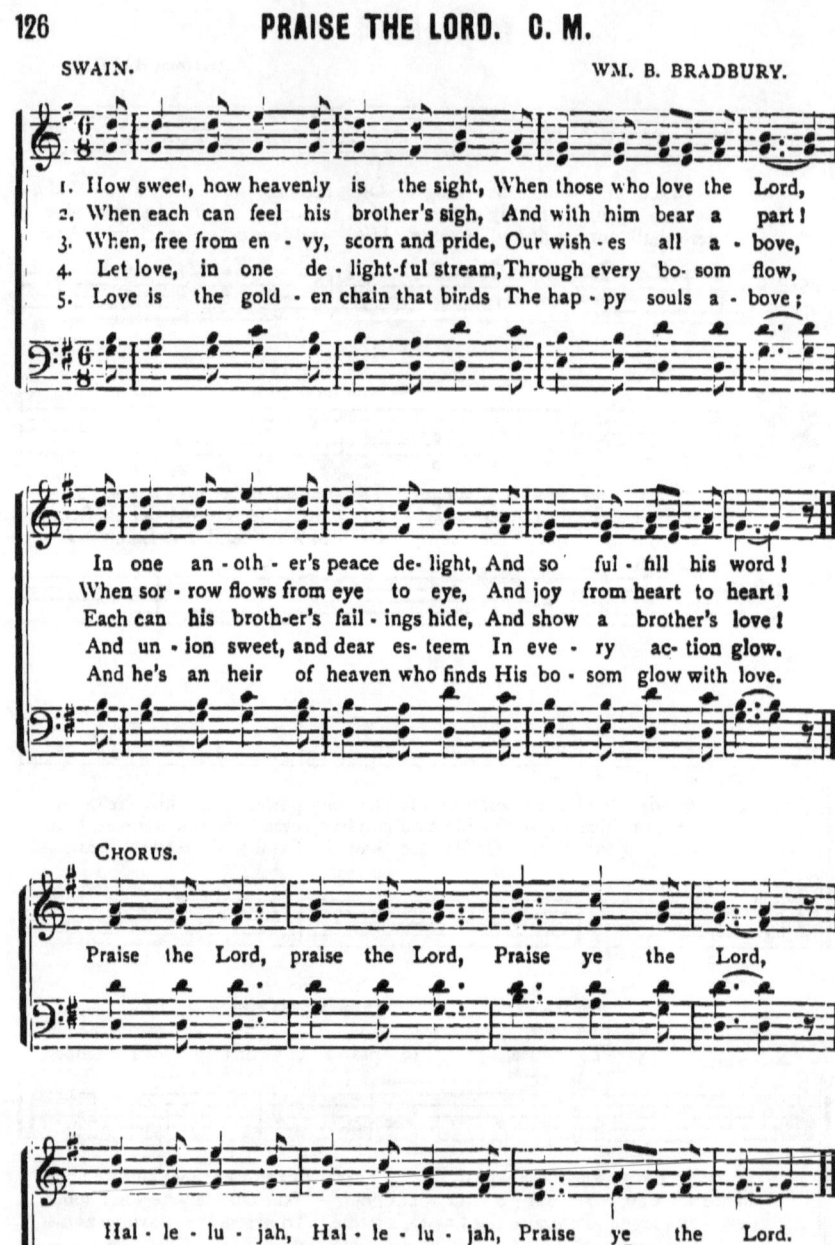

BENEATH THE SHADOW OF THY WING.

Mrs. T. M. GRIFFIN.　　　　　　　　　　　　　　　　　　　J. M. HUNT.

"Keep me as the apple of the eye, hide me under the shadow of thy wings."—Psa. 17: 8.

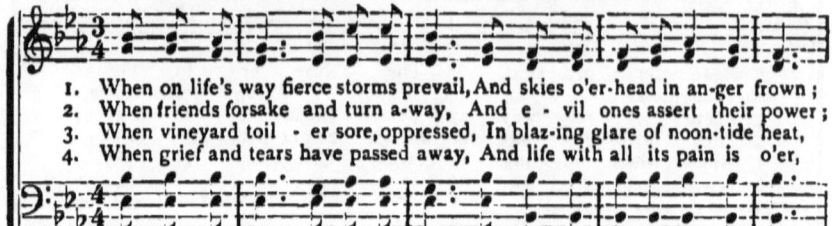

1. When on life's way fierce storms prevail, And skies o'er-head in an-ger frown;
2. When friends forsake and turn a-way, And e - vil ones assert their power;
3. When vineyard toil - er sore, oppressed, In blaz-ing glare of noon-tide heat,
4. When grief and tears have passed away, And life with all its pain is o'er,

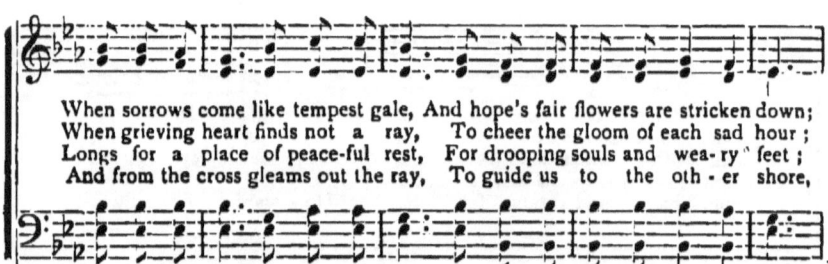

When sorrows come like tempest gale, And hope's fair flowers are stricken down;
When grieving heart finds not a ray, To cheer the gloom of each sad hour;
Longs for a place of peace-ful rest, For drooping souls and wea-ry feet;
And from the cross gleams out the ray, To guide us to the oth-er shore,

What can a trembling sin - ner do, But fly to Thee, un - mur-mur-ing,
What can a trembling sin - ner do, But fly to Thee, un - mur-mur-ing,
What can the faint-ing toil - er do, But fly to Thee, un - mur-mur-ing,
What will the ransomed spir- it do, But fly to Thee, and sweetly sing

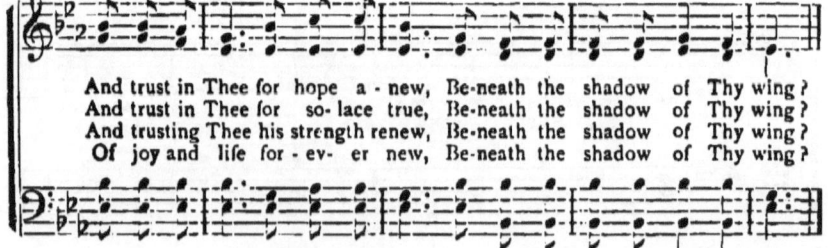

And trust in Thee for hope a - new, Be-neath the shadow of Thy wing?
And trust in Thee for so- lace true, Be-neath the shadow of Thy wing?
And trusting Thee his strength renew, Be-neath the shadow of Thy wing?
Of joy and life for - ev- er new, Be-neath the shadow of Thy wing?

BENEATH THE SHADOW OF THY WING.—Concluded.

Beneath the shadow, blessed shadow, Beneath the sha-dow of Thy wing;

We'll safe-ly rest, we'll safely rest, Beneath the shadow of Thy wing.

SILOAM. C. M.

Bishop HEBER.   I. B. WOODBURY.

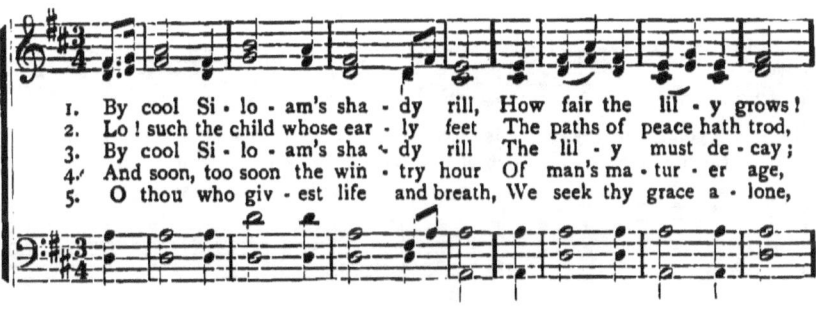

1. By cool Si-lo-am's sha-dy rill, How fair the lil-y grows!
2. Lo! such the child whose ear-ly feet The paths of peace hath trod,
3. By cool Si-lo-am's sha-dy rill The lil-y must de-cay;
4. And soon, too soon the win-try hour Of man's ma-tur-er age,
5. O thou who giv-est life and breath, We seek thy grace a-lone,

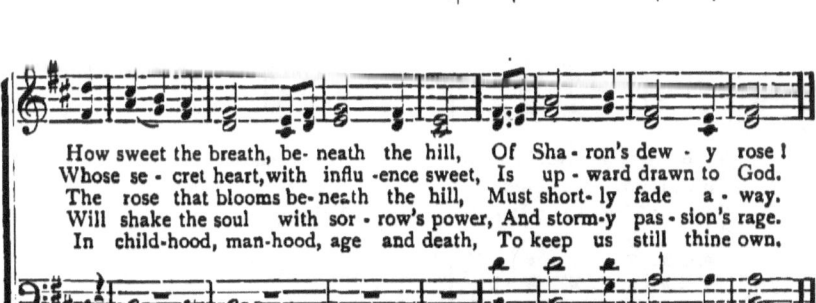

How sweet the breath, be-neath the hill, Of Sha-ron's dew-y rose!
Whose se-cret heart, with influ-ence sweet, Is up-ward drawn to God.
The rose that blooms be-neath the hill, Must short-ly fade a-way.
Will shake the soul with sor-row's power, And storm-y pas-sion's rage.
In child-hood, man-hood, age and death, To keep us still thine own.

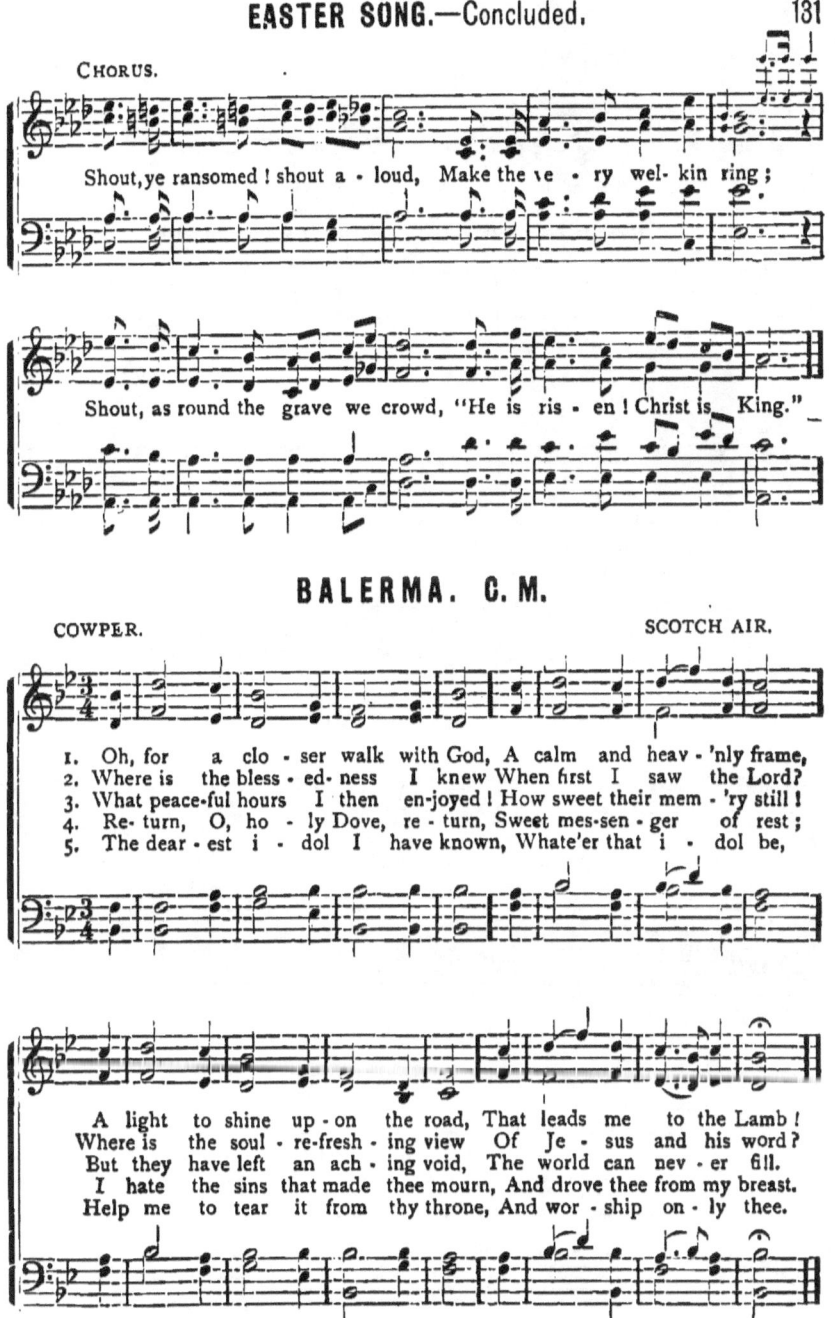

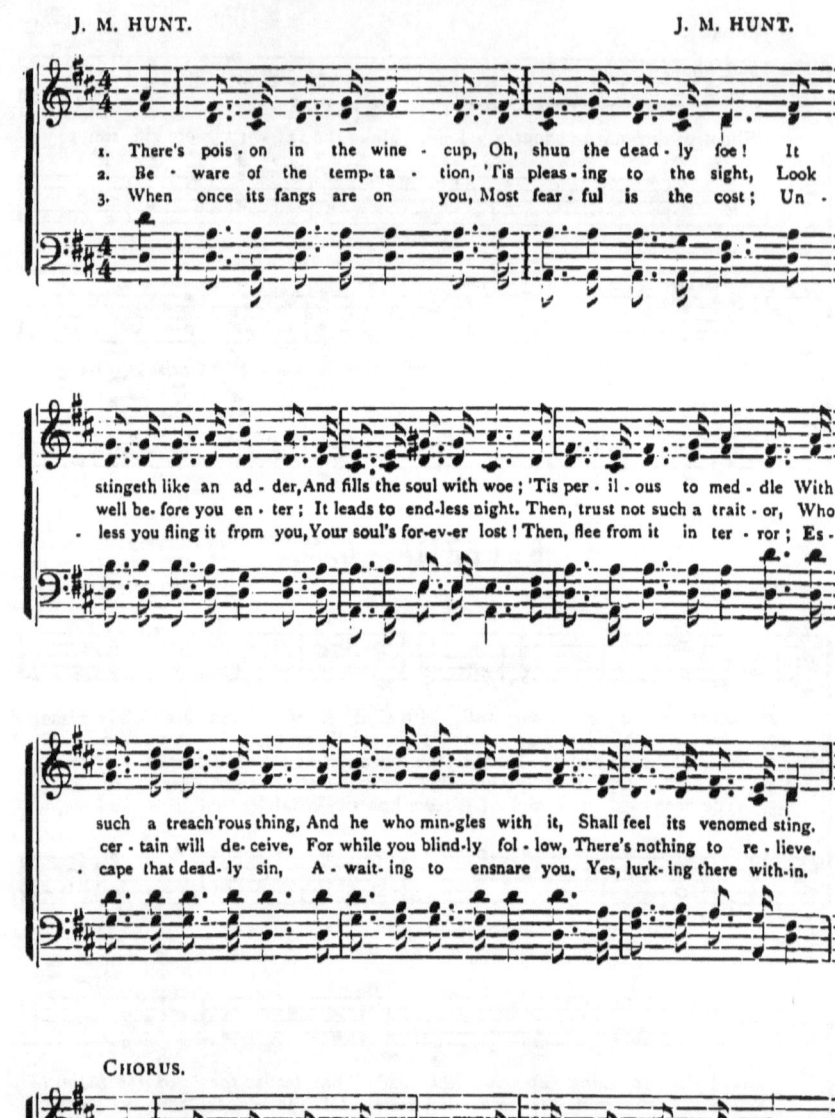

LOOK NOT ON THE WINE.—Concluded.

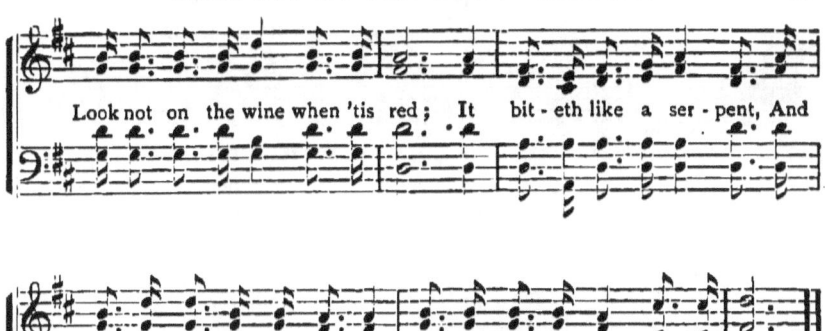

Look not on the wine when 'tis red; It bit-eth like a ser-pent, And sting-eth like an ad-der; Then, look not on the wine when 'tis red.

AZMON. C. M.

ISAAC WATTS.   C. G. GLASER.

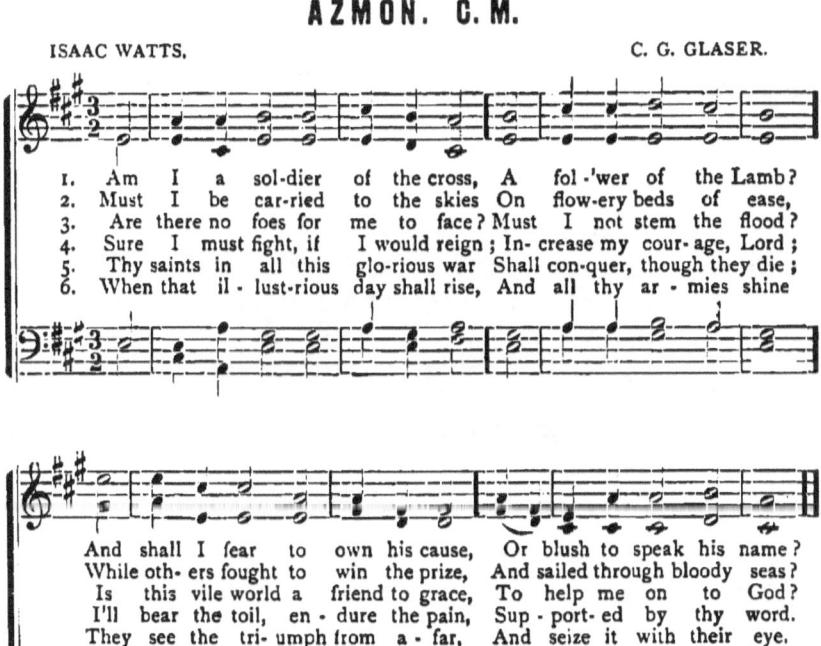

1. Am I a sol-dier of the cross, A fol-'wer of the Lamb?
2. Must I be car-ried to the skies On flow-ery beds of ease,
3. Are there no foes for me to face? Must I not stem the flood?
4. Sure I must fight, if I would reign; In-crease my cour-age, Lord,
5. Thy saints in all this glo-rious war Shall con-quer, though they die;
6. When that il-lust-rious day shall rise, And all thy ar-mies shine

And shall I fear to own his cause, Or blush to speak his name?
While oth-ers fought to win the prize, And sailed through bloody seas?
Is this vile world a friend to grace, To help me on to God?
I'll bear the toil, en-dure the pain, Sup-port-ed by thy word.
They see the tri-umph from a-far, And seize it with their eye.
In robes of vic-t'ry through the skies, The glo-ry shall be thine.

COME TO JESUS.

JOHN McPHERSON, by per.

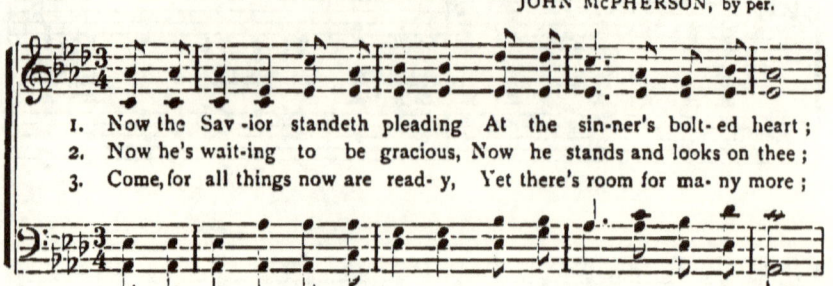

1. Now the Sav-ior standeth pleading At the sin-ner's bolt-ed heart;
2. Now he's wait-ing to be gracious, Now he stands and looks on thee;
3. Come, for all things now are read-y, Yet there's room for ma-ny more;

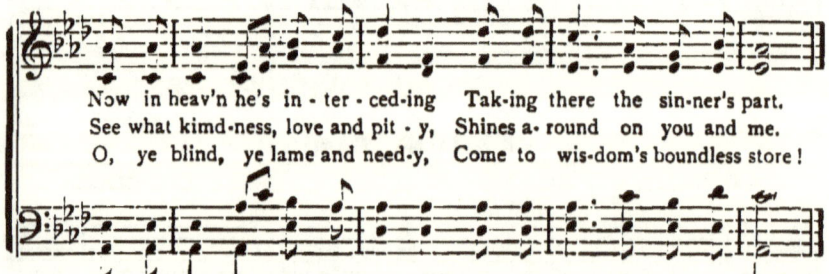

Now in heav'n he's in-ter-ced-ing Tak-ing there the sin-ner's part.
See what kimd-ness, love and pit-y, Shines a-round on you and me.
O, ye blind, ye lame and need-y, Come to wis-dom's boundless store!

CHORUS. Arranged.

Come to Je-sus, come to Je-sus, Come to Je-sus just now;

Just now come to Je-sus, Come to Je-sus just now.

MEAR. C. M.

ISSAC WATTS.

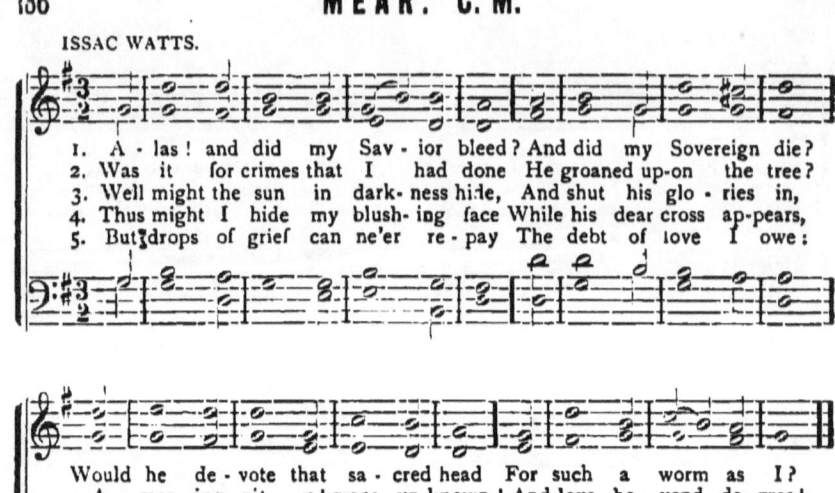

1. A-las! and did my Sav-ior bleed? And did my Sovereign die?
2. Was it for crimes that I had done He groaned up-on the tree?
3. Well might the sun in dark-ness hide, And shut his glo-ries in,
4. Thus might I hide my blush-ing face While his dear cross ap-pears,
5. But drops of grief can ne'er re-pay The debt of love I owe:

Would he de-vote that sa-cred head For such a worm as I?
A-maz-ing pit-y! grace un-known! And love be-yond de-gree!
When Christ, the might-y Mak-er, died For man the crea-ture's sin.
Dis-solve my heart in thank-ful-ness, And melt mine eyes to tears.
Here, Lord, I give my-self a-way; 'Tis all that I can do.

GRACE. 5th P. M.

I. B. WOODBURY.

1. 'Tis re-lig-ion that can give Sweet-est plea-sures while we live;
2. Aft-er death, its joys will be Last-ing as e-ter-ni-ty;

'Tis re-lig-ion must sup-ply Sol-id com-fort when we die.
Be the liv-ing God my Friend, Then my bliss shall nev-er end.

HARMONY GROVE. C. M. 137

NEWTON. *Moderato.* WM. WALKER.

1. A-maz-ing grace, how sweet the sound That saved a wretch like me!
2. 'Twas grace that taught my heart to fear, And grace my fears re-lieved;
3. Thro' ma-ny dan-gers, toils and snares, I have al-read-y come;

I once was lost, but now am found: Was blind, but now I see.
How pre-cious did that grace ap-pear, The hour I first be-lieved!
'Tis grace has brought me safe thus far, And grace will lead me home.

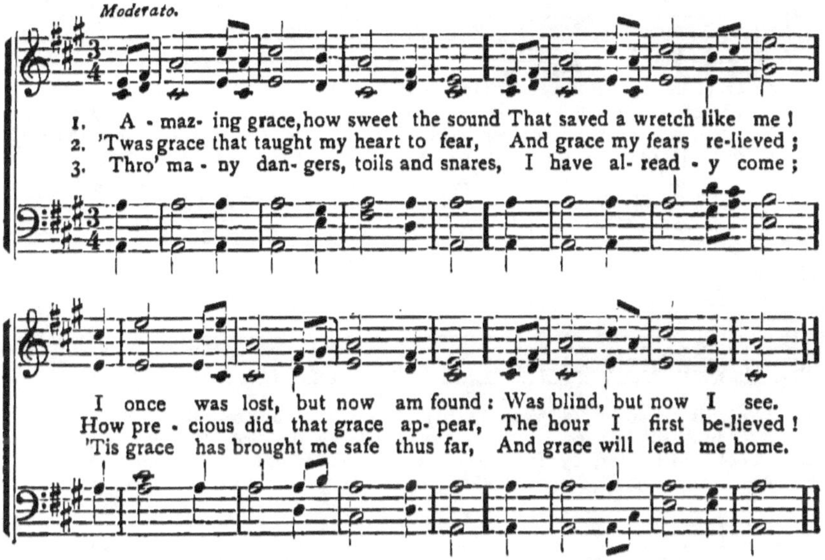

DENNIS. S. M.

Arr. from NAGELI.

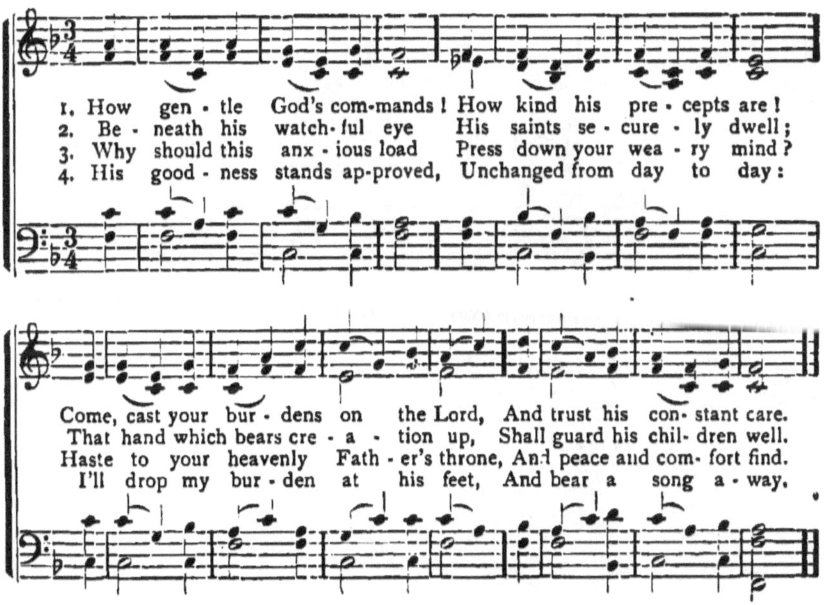

1. How gen-tle God's com-mands! How kind his pre-cepts are!
2. Be-neath his watch-ful eye His saints se-cure-ly dwell;
3. Why should this anx-ious load Press down your wea-ry mind?
4. His good-ness stands ap-proved, Unchanged from day to day:

Come, cast your bur-dens on the Lord, And trust his con-stant care.
That hand which bears cre-a-tion up, Shall guard his chil-dren well.
Haste to your heavenly Fath-er's throne, And peace and com-fort find.
I'll drop my bur-den at his feet, And bear a song a-way.

HENDON. 7s.

Dr. CHAS. MALAN.

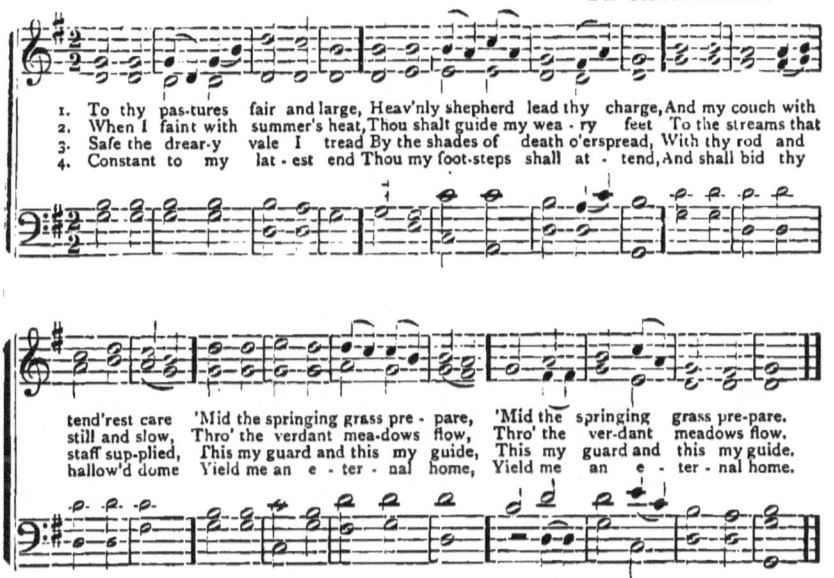

1. To thy pas-tures fair and large, Heav'nly shepherd lead thy charge, And my couch with tend'rest care 'Mid the springing grass pre-pare, 'Mid the springing grass pre-pare.
2. When I faint with summer's heat, Thou shalt guide my wea-ry feet To the streams that still and slow, Thro' the verdant mea-dows flow, Thro' the ver-dant meadows flow.
3. Safe the drear-y vale I tread By the shades of death o'erspread, With thy rod and staff sup-plied, This my guard and this my guide, This my guard and this my guide.
4. Constant to my lat-est end Thou my foot-steps shall at-tend, And shall bid thy hallow'd dome Yield me an e-ter-nal home, Yield me an e-ter-nal home.

EVAN. C. M.

RICE.
Rev. W. H. HAVERGAL.

Moderato.

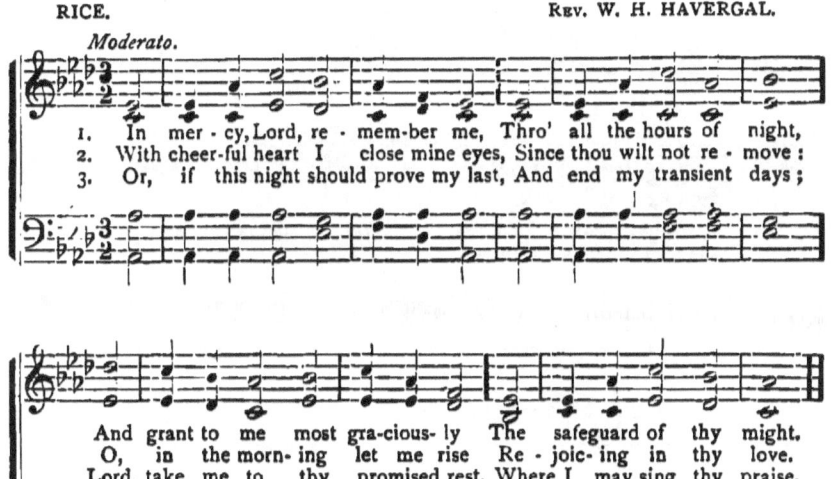

1. In mer-cy, Lord, re-mem-ber me, Thro' all the hours of night, And grant to me most gra-cious-ly The safeguard of thy might.
2. With cheer-ful heart I close mine eyes, Since thou wilt not re-move; O, in the morn-ing let me rise Re-joic-ing in thy love.
3. Or, if this night should prove my last, And end my transient days; Lord, take me to thy promised rest, Where I may sing thy praise.

Dr. T. HASTINGS.

bear the cross alone And all the world go free? No; there's a
re the saints above Who once went sorr'wing here, But now they
rat- ed cross I'll bear Till death shall set me free, And there go

one, And there's a cross for me, And there's a cross for me.
love, And joy without a tear, And joy without a tear.
o wear, For there's a crown for me, Oh, there's a crown for me.

WILLMARTH. L. M.

I. B. WOODBURY.

ey the wondrous cross On which the Prince of glo- ry died,
ord, that I should boast, Save in the death of Christ, my God;
head, his hands, his feet, Sor - row and love flow mingled down:
ealm of na- ture mine, That were a pre- sent far too small;

I count but loss, And pour contempt on all my pride.
s that charm me most, I sac - ri - fice them to his blood.
ve and sor-row meet, Or thorns com-pose so rich a crown!
-ing, so di - vine, Demands my soul, my life, my all.

AMERICA. 6s & 4s.

S. F. SMITH   NATIONAL AIR.

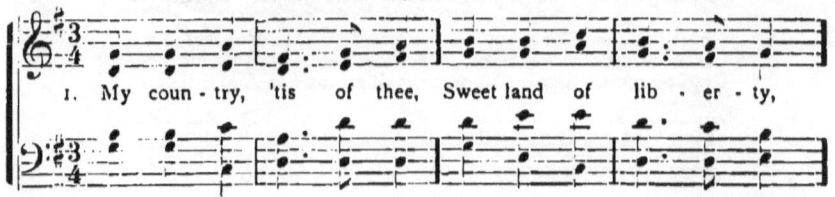

1.
My country, 'tis of thee,
Sweet land of liberty,
  Of thee I sing ;
Land where my fathers died,
Land of the pilgrim's pride,
From ev'ry mountain side
  Let freedom ring.

2.
My native country, thee—
Land of the noble, free—
  Thy name I love ;
I love thy rocks and rills,
Thy woods and templed hills ;
My heart with rapture thrills
  Like that above.

3.
Let music swell the breeze,
And ring from all the trees
  Sweet freedom's song :
Let mortal tongues awake ;
Let all that breathe partake ;
Let rocks their silence break—
  The sound prolong.

4.
Our fathers' God, to thee,
Author of liberty,
  To thee we sing ;
Long may our land be bright
With freedom's holy light ;
Protect us by thy might,
  Great God, our King.

LET IT PASS. 143

But I say unto you that ye resist not evil.—MATT. 5: 39.

Words Arr. by MRS. T. M. GRIFFIN. L. B. SHOOK.

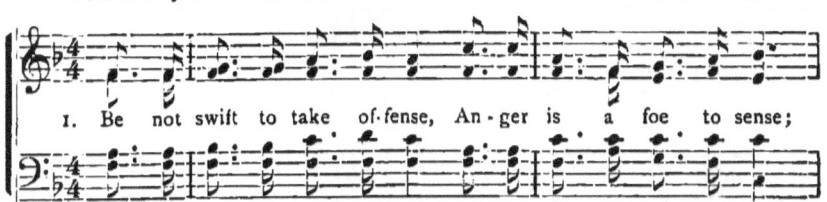

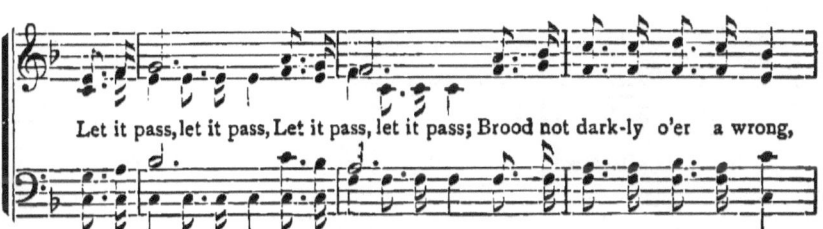

1.

Be not swift to take offence,
Anger is a foe to sense,
  Let it pass, let it pass.
Brood not darkly o'er a wrong,
It will disappear ere long,
  Let it pass, let it pass.

2.

Echo not an angry word,
Think how often you have erred;
  Let it pass, let it pass.
Since our joys must pass away,
Why, then, should our sorrows stay?
  Let it pass, let it pass.

3.

If for good, you're given ill,
O! be kind and gentle still;
  Let it pass, let it pass.
Let us not resent, but wait,
And our triumph will be great;
  Let it pass, let it pass.

4.

Bid unpleasant thoughts depart;
Lay these kindly words to heart,
  Let it pass, let it pass.
Better to be wronged, than wrong,
Therefore sing this cheering song,
  Let it pass, let it pass.

THE LORD'S PRAYER.

L. B. SHOOK.

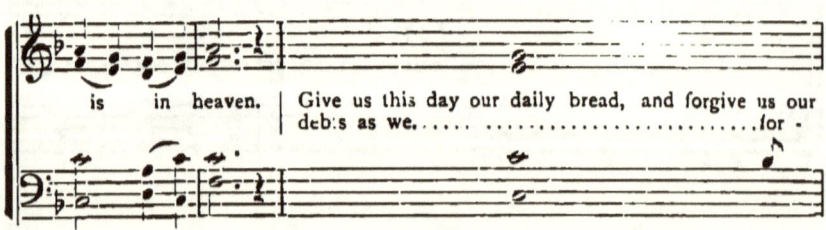
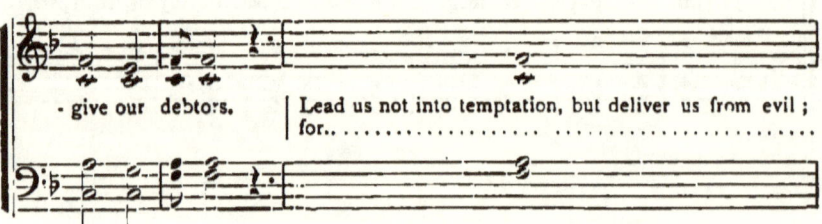

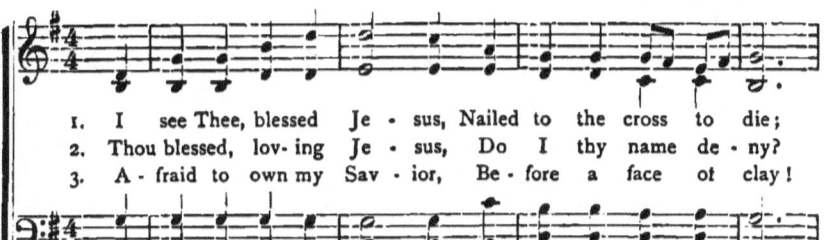
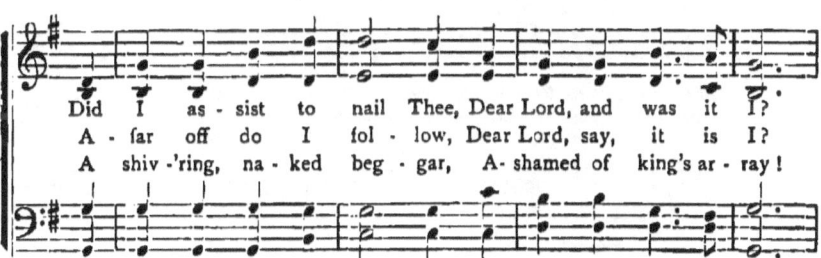
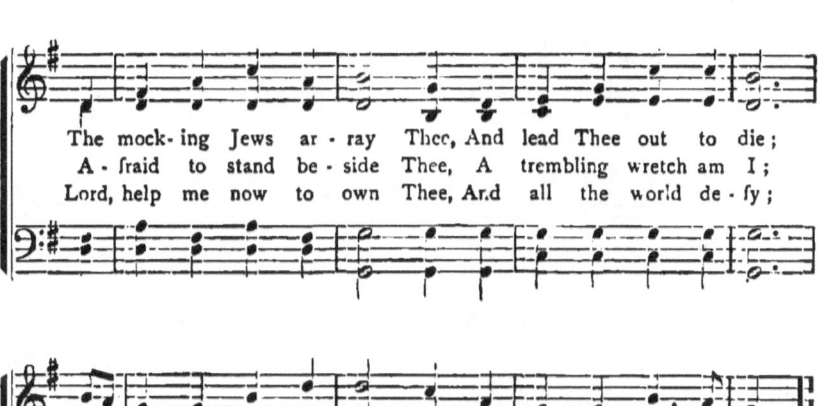
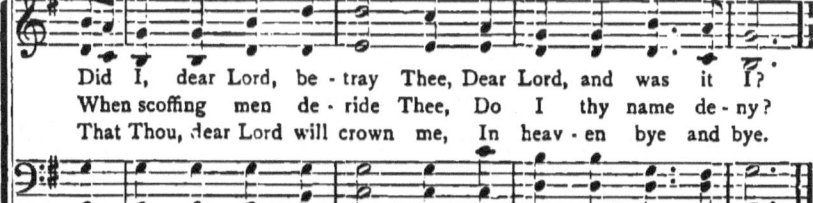

PEACE ON THE OTHER SIDE.

CHAS. B. HOLMES.

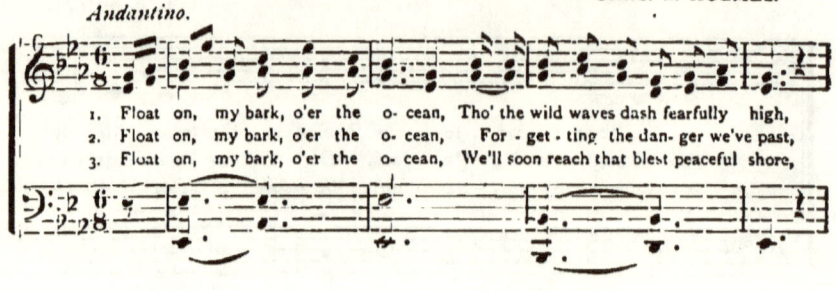

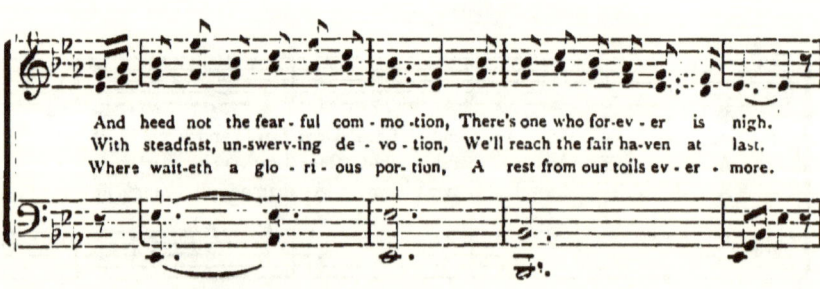

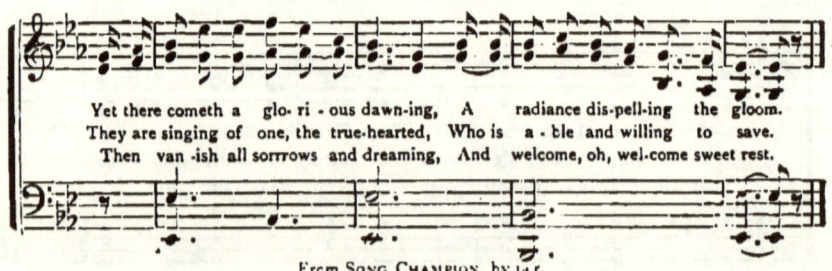

From Song Champion, by ber.

PEACE ON THE OTHER SIDE.—Concluded.

147

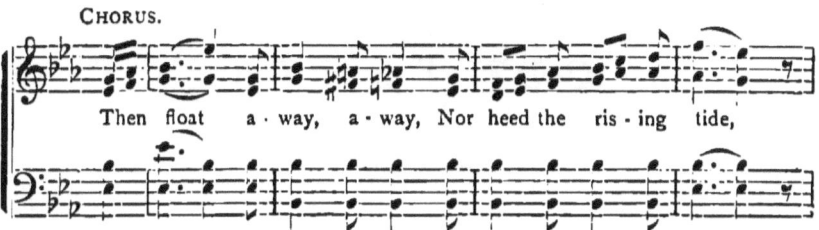

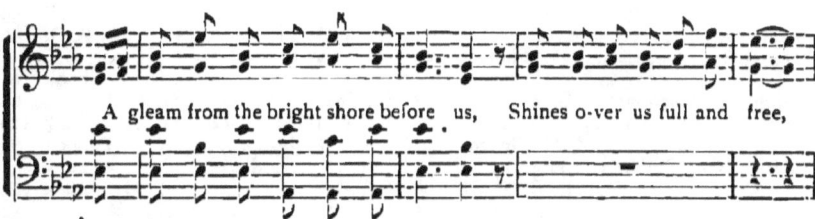
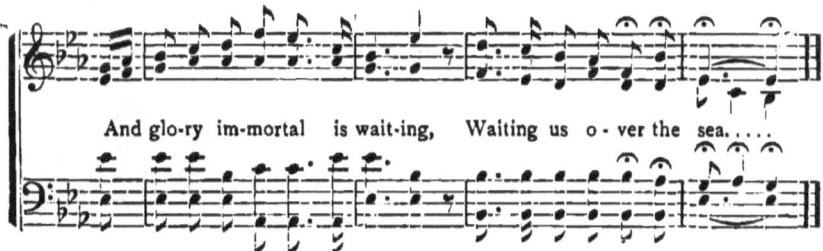

CONTENTS.

	PAGE		PAGE
America............National Air	142	Give Praise to the Lord..F. L. Hunt	106
Anthony............J. W. Williams	60	Gladsome Land (The)....McPherson	28
Austin..............Kate Robbins	35	Glad To-morrow (The)..J. M. Hunt	83
Autumn................	123	Glorious Day When Christ Shall	
Azmon. C. M........C. G. Glaser	133	Come............L. B. Shook	63
		Glory Be to God........J. M. Hunt	81
Balerma. C. M..................	131	God's Word..........C. E. Pollock	76
Beautiful City. L. M....T. J. Cook	140	Golden City (The)......L. B. Shook	101
Beautiful Morning......L. B. Shook	79	Good Night................Scotch	111
Beautiful Robe..........L. B. Shook	112	Go, Tell the Joyful Story.....Bell	96
Be Guiding Me...Mrs. T. M. Griffin	37	Grace. 5th P. M....I. B. Woodbury	136
Beneath the Shadow of Thy Wing...			
.................J. M. Hunt	128	Happy Land (The)....C. E. Pollock	42
Bethany. 6s and 4s....Lowell Mason	127	Harmony Grove. C. M..Wm. Walker	137
Be Still, My Heart, and Wait........		Harwell..............Lowell Mason	124
....................L. B. Shook	10	Hendon. 7s..........Chas. Malan	139
Beyond the Dim Shores of Time....		Holland............Allie L. Smith	19
.................L. B. S.	100	How Firm a Foundation...........	94
Bless the Little Lambs....J. M. Hunt	5		
Blow Ye the Trumpet..Geo. F. Root	69	I Believe.............L. B. Shook	59
Boone.........................	97	I Lay My Sins on Jesus.....L. B. S.	86
By and By..........McPherson	29	I'll Away to the Sunday School.....	
		....................Shook	95
Children's Hosannas....L. B. Shook	87	I'll Bear the Cross....H. N. Lincoln	66
Come and Bless Us........L. B. S.	49	I Need the Love of Jesus.....Shook	110
Come To Jesus..........McPherson	134	I Now Believe........C. E. Pollock	64
Come to Our Father's House.......		In the Vineyard..............Shook	38
....................L. B. Shook	108	Is It I?....................Shook	145
Clime of the Blest........L. B. S.	55	It Is Finished...... .....J. M. Hunt	50
Crown of Life..........F. L. Hunt	90	It Is Not Death to Die..L. B. Shook	11
Closing Song..........L. B. Shook	91	I Would Love Thee....Geo. F. Root	67
De Fleury...............De Fleury	122	Jesus Knows and Cares for Me......	
Dennis. S. M............Nagell	137	...................H. N. Lincoln	39
Easter Song..........L. B. Shook	130	Keep Me...... ....J. M. Hunt	105
Evan. C. M...........Havergal	139	Kentucky. S. M.......Old melody	138
Flow On..........F. L. Hunt	103	Land That's Far Away (The).......	
Following On............L. B. S.	104	...................L. B. Shook	45
For Christ To-day......J. M. Hunt	53	Let It Pass.... ....L. B. S.	143
Fount of Grace.....G. W. Grammer	62	Let Me Tarry at the Fountain......	
Fresno................L. B. Shook	27	...................J. M. Hunt	12

	PAGE		PAGE
Light for One Step More..J. M. Hunt	22	Saint's Home...............Shook	107
Lingering Near....Mrs. T. M. Griffin	58	Savior Is Calling For Thee.........	
Look Not on the Wine...J. M. Hunt	132	............T. W. Dennington	56
Lord Is Near..........L. B. Shook	109	Save, Lord, Save......L. B. Shook	61
Lord's Prayer..............L. B. S.	144	Savior, Lead Us All the Way..Shook	33
Love Ye One Another....J. M. Hunt	85	Seek a Savior's Blessing..........	
		................Allie L. Smith	121
Malone...............L. B. Shook	99	Seeking the Lost Sheep..J. M. Hunt	46
McCreary..........Allie L. Smith	23	Siloam. C. M......I. B. Woodbury	129
Mear. C. M......................	136	Singing All the Way....L. B. Shook	98
Merry Christmas.......J. R. Murray	74	Sing, Children, Sing........L. B. S.	77
Morning Light Is Breaking.........		Sing of His Love...........Shook	120
..................L. B. Shook	52	Stay, Weary Child....C. E. Pollock	48
Morning Prayer............L. B. S	31	Sunday School Army....L. B. Shook	78
My Crown of Righteousness........		Sutton...........................	93
..............T. Martin Towne	24	Sweet Galilee.........C. E. Pollock	71
My Home Above...Jas. McGranahan	4	Sweet Haven of Rest..C. E. Pollock	102
Nearing My Home......L. B. Shook	118	Tell Jesus.............L. B. Shook	17
Nelson. C. M........Allie L. Smith	25	Temperance Song..........L. B. S.	14
No Night On That Golden Shore....		There Is Joy..............Shook	116
..................L. B. Shook	8	There's A Song In the Air..L. B. S.	80
		To the Arms of Jesus....J. M. Hunt	72
O, Heaven, Sweet Heaven..........		Transient..............L. B. Shook	13
................John McPherson	70	Trust...................L. B. S.	82
O, Heart, Was It In Vain?.........		Trust In Jesus.......H. N. Lincoln	6
....................J. M. Hunt	43	Trust On............L. B. Shook	47
Oh, Yes, I Will Come to The Savior.			
..................L. B. S.	114	Union.............P. H. Montague	7
On the Banks Of That Bright River..		Up There In Heaven....L. B. Shook	36
....................L. B. S.	34		
Open the Door for the Children.....		Varina. C. M...............Rink	135
..................Shook	30	Vaughn..........Daniel P. Airhart	21
Ortonville. C. M....Dr. Hastings	141		
Our Savior's Name.....L. B. Shook	16	Walking Life's Sea......McPherson	44
Over the Beautiful Hills..J. B. Herbert	88	Was It In Vain?............Shook	92
		Way Is Long and Weary (The).....	
Peace On the Other Side...........		....................J. M. Hunt	115
............Charles B. Holmes	146	We Are Coming........C. E. Leslie	41
Pearly Gate (The)......L. B. Shook	57	We're Going Home...Allie L. Smith	75
Pass Along the Watchword..L. B. S.	118	We Come With Happy Songs......	
Praise the Lord. C. M...........		................L. B. Shook	3
..............Wm. B. Bradbury	126	We Will Go..........G. W. Lyon	20
Precious Things.......C. E. Pollock	68	What Can Children Do?...........	
Praising Jesus......John McPherson	40	................J. G. Burdick	54
		What Mean Those Holy Voices?....	
Remember the Savior...L. B. Shook	32	..................Shook	119
Rest.....................L. B. S.	26	When We Meet... ....L. B. S.	84
Retreat. L. M.......Dr. Hastings	138	Who Will Greet Me First In Heaven?	
		................L. B. Shook	18
Sabbath Praises........L. B. Shook	73	Williams..................Haydn	125
Safely There............J. M. Hunt	65	Willmarth. L. M..I. B. Woodbury	141
Sailing Into Port...........L. B.S.	51		

The King of Piano Methods.
BRAINARD'S
New Method for Piano-Forte,
By George W. Brainard.

To which is added the celebrated "Musical Hints" to teachers, pupils and parents, and the "Elements of Harmony," by Dr. Karl Merz.

Brainard's New Method has become the standard piano instruction book in this country and is used in preference to all others by the leading teachers. It has recently been enlarged, revised and improved, and stands to-day at the head of piano-forte methods. It is a complete work, yet contains no useless matter, every page being useful and available. Thousands of teachers are using it, and from the immense number of testimonials we have received we have only room to present the following:

FROM PROMINENT TEACHERS.

——I find BRAINARD'S NEW METHOD the most comprehensive work of the kind. I use it with my scholars with best results. For new beginners it is unequaled.
C. F. Boos, Tiffin, O.

——I take great pleasure in certifying that having used BRAINARD'S NEW METHOD with my pupils. I find it equal to any method I have ever used.
Mrs. S. M. Kemp, Tiffin, O.

——I take pleasure in recommending BRAINARD'S NEW METHOD FOR THE PIANO. I consider it a most valuable addition to the many methods already published. The rudiments of music are given in the clearest possible manner, the pupil is not advanced without being thoroughly prepared for it. One clef is given at a time, and continued until the pupil has become familiar with the notes belonging to this staff. The scales are not introduced early, thus giving the scholar time to attain to some degree of power. It is progressive. Just such a work as intelligent teachers have long desired.
Mrs. Nettie S. Gettle, New London, O.

——We find that BRAINARD'S NEW METHOD FOR THE PIANO sells readily wherever teachers give it a trial. The Sisters of the Convent use it now in preference to any other.
S. Morrison, Bradford, Pa.

——We have handled your piano method during the past year. A number of our teachers and Sisters of the Convent are using it and speak in its favor. We have good reason to believe it will be one of the *leading* books in this section.
W. C Burgess, Auburn N. Y.

——I am using your BRAINARD'S NEW METHOD FOR THE PIANO and can safely say it gives the most complete satisfaction, especially to beginners. I prefer it to any I have ever used.
Mrs. C. A. Abbey, Rochester, N. Y.

——I have examined and used BRAINARD'S NEW METHOD FOR THE PIANO and find it excellently adapted to the wants of teachers and students. The exercises are progressive and enable pupils gradually to overcome all technical difficulties. The recreations are interesting and illustrate various styles of composition, and finally a thorough study of the work cannot fail to lay the foundation on which and from which may be developed a pianist of the highest order. Robert Denton, of Denton & Cottier, Buffalo, N. Y.

——I have discontinued all other methods and use yours only.
Louis Hast, Louisville, Ky.

——It is thoroughly practical and progressive and contains no useless matter.
Chas. Kinkel, Shelbyville, Ky.

——I recommend it to teachers and students as superior to any work of the kind.
Wm. Heydler, Cleveland, O.

——Much more progressive and complete than Richardsons's or Peters' method.
Wm. Bendix, Cleveland, O.

——It is *the* instruction book of the day. Accept my sincere congratulations.
Addie Weed.

——Having examined BRAINARD'S NEW METHOD FOR THE PIANO-FORTE, I take pleasure in saying that in many respects it is superior to any other of the kind gotten up in this country.
J. C. Cook, New York.

PRICE $3.00, MAILED POST-PAID.

New and Enlarged Edition.

HERBERT'S
MALE QUARTET AND CHORUS BOOK.

A superb collection of Quartets and Choruses for Men's voices. The variety and excellence of the music in this book will win for it a popularity seldom equalled. It is suitable for use in the GLEE CLUB, CONCERT ROOM, COLLEGE, CHURCH AND HOME, as will be seen by a glance at the following list of contents:

A Few More Years shall Roll............	Sleepest thou still, Mine Own.............
A Love Song...........................	Sleep, Fairest, Sleep......................
Angel of Patience......................	Sleep, Sweetest, Sleep....................
A Social Drink.........................	Social Drink.............................
Awake! the Starry Midnight hour........	Soft o'er the Fountain....................
Behold the Morning Gleaming...........	Solemn Midnight.........................
Better late than Never..................	Solomon Ray—Chant ....
Boat Song.............................	Soldier's Farewell........................
Brother, thou art gone to Rest	So the Story Goes........................
Clouds of the Summer Night.............	Song of the Skaters......................
Dirge for a Child.......................	Song Prayer.............................
Decoration Song........................	Stand Firm..............................
Evening Bells..........................	Swing Low, Sweet Chariot.................
Farewell...............................	Tell me some Certain Sign................
Farewell, my Native Land...............	The Brook whose Flow...................
Gideon's Band.........................	The College Bell.........................
God is in His Holy Temple...............	The Deep, Deep Sea......................
Go to thy Rest in Peace.................	The Greeting............................
Hail, Hail.............................	The Huntsmen's Farewell.................
Hang up his Harp, he'll wake no more.....	The Hymns my Mother Sung.............
How fair the Maiden....................	The Lone Cottage........................
How goes the Money....................	The Merry Sugar Making.................
Huzza! the Cause Speeds On.	The Name in the Sand....................
I loved a Lass, a Fair One................	The Old Church Bell.....................
In the Cross of Christ I Glory	The Old Days of the War.................
I've been a-list'ning all de Night...........	The Publican's Defense ....
Ladies' Tobacco Song...................	The Sailor's Boy's Grave..................
Lady, Farewell	The Singer's March.......................
Lay me Where my Mother Sleeps.........	The Summer Rain.......................
Let Him Rest..........................	The Temperance Cause...................
Look! Neighbors, Look!—Catch..........	The Three Chafers.......................
Mercy's Door..........................	The Torpedo and the Whale...............
More and More........................	The Winter has Passed...................
My Boyhood...........................	The Withered Autumn Leaves, &c........
My Cigar..............................	The Voyage.............................
My Old Ox-team.......................	There's Music in a Mother's Voice ....
Nancy Lee.............................	Touch not the Wine......................
Oh, de Hebben is Shinin'................	Twanging his Sweet Guitar................
Oh, Wasn't dat a Wide Riber............	'Twas You Sir—Catch....................
Peace, be Still.........................	Walk You in de Light....................
Rocking on the Billows of the Deep.......	We are Happy and Tree..................
Rowing Swiftly down the Stream.........	We meet Again, Boys ....
Serenade..............................	When a Man's a little bit Poorly..........
Singing time to Sleep...................	Who will Stand for Fatherland............

Price 60 cents per copy. $6.00 per dozen. Sample copy 60 cents.

The King of Reed Organ Instruction Books!

KARL MERZ'
Modern Method for Parlor Organ.

Now the leading, best and most popular book in use. It is endorsed by thousands of teachers and musicians, and generally admitted superior to all others, as an instruction book for Reed Organs. It was written by a practical teacher, is very progressive, and every point is made plain to both teacher and pupil. The selections, both vocal and instrumental, are unusually attractive, and a plain course on Harmony closes the book. We have only room for a few of the thousands of testimonials received :

MRS. STELLA P. SARJENT, music teacher in Perdue University, Lafayette, Ind., says: I have used all the popular organ instruction books, but have never found one so thorough and satisfactory as "Merz' Modern Organ Method." I use it exclusively now, and am happy to recommend it to all teachers and pupils.

MISS JENNIE J. BROWN, music teacher at Middleford, O., says : I am using "Merz' Improved Modern Method for the Parlor Organ," and like it very much. I like the plan of teaching rythms the first thing, also the way of introducing flats and sharps alternately.

FRED. F. LEWIS, teacher, Jamestown, Wis., writes: I like "Merz' Organ Method" so well that I have introduced it among my scholars, and it gives perfect satisfaction. I think it far ahead of any other organ instructor. The exercises are graded in such an easy and natural order, and at the same time are so thorough, pleasing and instructive, that the dullest pupil, by careful practice, will become interested, and the amusements are such as to give them a taste for better music than any other book that I use.

MISS FANNY O'BYRNE, a prominent teacher in Brookville, Ind., writes: I like it very much. Think the explanations more thorough and clear than those of any other book I have seen. Any one old enough to understand what they read, can almost learn without a teacher.

C. M. VON MEREDITH, Marengo, O., says - As an instruction book for beginners it is unequaled and I recommend it without hesitation to those desirous of making rapid progress in the art of organ playing.

MISS LUELLA CASEY, of Patoka, Ind., writes: I have used Karl Merz' Instruction Book for the Reed Organ, and find it to be a superior Book to any I have seen. The rudiments are simple enough for the dullest pupil, the exercises progress systematically, giving the teacher sufficient material to work with, and the amusements are attractive and pleasing. I heartily recommend the book.

We invite a critical examination of "Karl Merz' Organ Method," feeling confident that any teacher, who carefully compares it with the numerous old-fashion organ books in the market (many of them compiled by persons that evidently do not understand the first principles of the organ), will agree with us that no such organ method has before been presented to the musical public. "Karl Merz' Method" can be obtained through any music dealer and examined at any first-class music store, or a copy will be sent post-paid on receipt of price.

Price $2.50.

Contains 172 pages, elegantly printed on heavy tinted paper, firmly bound and with red edges.

www.ingramcontent.com/pod-product-compliance
Lightning Source LLC
Chambersburg PA
CBHW030340170426
43202CB00010B/1185